UNDER EDUCATED

7 Life Lessons Schools FORGOT to Teach Us

Derrick J. Love

ISBN: 978-0-9891941-2-9 (paperback)

TABLE OF CONTENTS

ABOUT THE AUTHOR

Derrick J. Love is on a mission to empower and educate others with the knowledge and wisdom he has gained through many of life's teaching moments. He was born and raised in a small farm town in Louisiana where opportunities were slim and poverty was the norm. Being raised by a single mom with 5 other siblings helped to shape and cultivate his drive to escape poverty and create a better life for himself. The journey wasn't easy or smooth. But, in spite of the many challenges life presented, he has managed to accomplish many things once thought to be beyond his reach or capacity.

Under-Educated is Derrick's second book. The first book titled *Unlock Your Mind... Unlock Your Money* has changed the lives of readers all over the world. As his passion for and confidence in his message that "in order to change your financial future, you first have to change your mentality and mindset" was fueled by the success of the first book, he began to share his message of Unlock Your Mind at colleges, high schools, and churches. Derrick has also shared the Unlock Your Mind message in corporate America with large companies like Phillips 66 Oil and Gas as well as large corporate conferences. His unique and practical approach to personal finances has made him a favorite for conferences and workshops where finances are a topic of discussion.

Derrick is an active real estate broker in the Houston, TX area where he has helped hundreds of clients build wealth through real estate ownership and investments. He owns several investment rental properties. He is also a trained personal finance coach who has helped many people take back control of their personal finances, pay off thousands of dollars in debt, increase their savings, create an investment plan, and increase their income simply by helping them to see their short-term sacrifices are worth it to achieve their long-term goals of financial freedom.

Derrick has been married for 20 years and has two beautiful children. Being a father is one of his most sacred titles and one of the greatest accomplishments of his life. Derrick feels a great burden to share the things he has learned in life with the world in hopes of helping others unlock their true potential and experience all that life has for them.

INTRODUCTION

"Derrick! Derrick, wake up! Get up boy! It's time for school and you better not miss that bus!" Those were the words breaking through the walls of my bedroom as my mom's voice echoed down the hall and interrupted my sleep. I popped out of my bed like a soldier on the first day of bootcamp. "Yes ma'am. I'm up". Once I fully gained consciousness and became aware of why I was awakened with such hostility, a new excitement came over me with the realization that I was about to embark upon a new journey in life. I was going to school. Woo-hoo!

I'd heard so many good things about school and I couldn't wait to experience them all for myself. My mom had repeatedly emphasized how excited she was that I was finally going to school. At the time, I wasn't sure why she was so excited to be sending me away from home. I just figured school had to be a great place for her to be that excited about me leaving and going somewhere else all day.

I was also excited because I had brand new clothes that my mom had finally gotten out of layaway a few days before school started but had forbidden me to wear until the first day of school. I couldn't wait to finally put my new clothes on. This was the first time I had gotten a lot of new clothes at one time. So, I'm not sure if I was more excited about school itself and all the things I would learn or being able to wear my new clothes. Either way, I was excited. "Kindergarten, here I come". I had new clothes, a fresh haircut and my face shined like a brand-new penny from all the Vaseline my mom had smeared over it in preparation for my big day. Off I went. The journey had begun!

I must say, the first year was a pretty cool experience. I was able to meet some new friends and I'm pretty sure I learned a lot of fundamental, educational stuff like the art of coloring within the lines, learning to write the alphabet, doing basic math, etc.

As I matriculated through school, I repeated this pattern for the next 12 years. Nine out of twelve months of my entire year was spent sitting in a classroom. Each year started with the same excitement. There was something about the newness of starting school. Perhaps it was because that's when I would get new clothes. Or maybe it was when I got a chance to see all my old friends. Whatever the reason was, I was always excited about the beginning of school. But then somewhere around the middle of the school year, after the clothes were no longer new, and my friends had run out of exciting stories to tell from their summer break, and school had become more about doing homework, I realized that I hated learning a bunch of seemingly useless information. Of course, I appreciated the core curriculum which included mathematics, reading, writing and spelling – all of which were essential. I even appreciated learning about American history, Geography, Science, Chemistry and Biology throughout my pilgrimage of K-12, public education. But I was soon to discover that all the teaching I was receiving wasn't enough. I was still UNDER-EDUCATED when it came to being prepared to function in day-to-day life as an adult.

Those years in the classroom taught me how to be a good student, how to remember data for an exam and how to follow the rules in a structured environment. They prepared me for the workplace. But they didn't prepare me for life outside of school where I would spend the majority of my time trying to function.

After graduating high school and entering the world for the first time as an adult, I quickly realized just how little I'd learned in school about real life, how little I'd learned about people, how little I'd learned about personal finances and how money works, and how little I'd learned about basic things like buying a home or investing in the stock market to build wealth. I was well prepared to take a reading comprehension exam and I could memorize formulas to solve math problems, but life taught me those skills alone were not in high demand in the real world. In real life, a good portion of what I'd learned in school was not applicable. It was years later, after life had beat the crap out of me, that I realized just how UNDER-EDUCATED I was about functioning outside of the classroom.

I'm sure there are plenty of lessons the schools don't teach the average public education student. But, for the purpose of this book, I will talk about 7 life lessons I deem to be important for having a purposeful, meaningful, holistic and well-balanced life you can be proud to live. I genuinely believe if I had the insights from the lessons I'm about to talk about as a young teenager or young adult, I would have avoided many of the mistakes I made that set me back both financially and emotionally. Thus, I decided to write this book in hopes of helping many people get a head start in life and avoid some of the mistakes I made simply due to my ignorance (lack of knowledge).

In the event of turbulence

Before we get to lesson ONE, allow me to share a story with you for a moment. On a flight a few years ago, I encountered some pretty frightening turbulence. In case this word is foreign to you, turbulence is when an airplane encounters rough air while flying that causes the plane to shake and shift seemingly uncontrollably. There are sudden drops in altitude that make you feel like you're falling out of the sky. It can be very disturbing and scary, especially for someone like myself who's afraid of heights. Usually, when the plane is about to encounter turbulence, the pilot will come on the air and let the passengers know what to expect. For people like me, this warning is appreciated. It lets me know the pilot is aware of the situation and the pilot has it under control.

Some turbulence is expected on a flight. But all turbulence is not created equal, and some turbulence is worse than others. This particular trip, I was enroute to New York when we encountered turbulence and I was flying from Houston, TX. The turbulence was so bad, I vowed if and when the plane landed, I was going to go to the nearest rental car location, rent me a car and drive my butt back home. I determined that where I was going was not worth me dying trying to get there. And to make matters worse, the pilot didn't even tell us ahead of time to brace ourselves. There is no greater sense of helplessness than being thirty thousand feet above ground in an airplane that you can't fly. So, I made peace in my mind and concluded I had lived the best life I could using what I had to work with. I thought to myself silently as I was praying, "I hope I was a great father, friend, husband..." etc. The two to three minutes of turbulence felt like an eternity.

Once the plane passed through the rough air and things began to smooth back out, it dawned on me. We are doing something that goes against the natural laws of gravity. We're not supposed to even be up here. This act defies nature. It's not normal. There's nothing natural about a huge chunk of metal being able to elevate and maintain itself in the air. Let alone carry hundreds of people. Yet, that's exactly what we were doing – we were flying!

I started to think about all the planes that travel daily. I thought about the extremely low percentage of planes historically that have crashed compared to the ones that reach their destination safely. As I reflected on this reality, I was able to calm my nerves enough to continue on the journey to my final destination to Ghana Africa. I started to realize that over 97 percent of the flight was pretty smooth as we glided through the air at 400 miles per hour. If I had aborted my trip and turned around based upon the small 3 percent of the flight that was turbulent or uncomfortable, what would I have missed out on? I would have missed out on an amazing experience of a lifetime to hang out in Africa for 10 days, meet some amazing people, eat some delicious food and experiencing things you can only get in Africa.

Why did I share that story with you? I'm very passionate about helping people succeed in life using the life experiences that I've gained over the years, both good and bad. As a Dave Ramsey trained Personal Finance Coach and licensed Texas Real Estate Broker, I'm often tasked with giving advice and counsel to my clients that may not be the easiest to digest, but it may be the best solution to get them to a better place in life financially. At times as a coach, I may take a strong stance in certain areas based on my personal knowledge and experiences, but my advice and guidance are always designed to serve the best interest of my clients. You are now my client and you're about to go on a journey with me. I'm excited to have the opportunity to share some of the lessons I've learned in life that weren't taught to me in any formal educational setting. However, I want to give you a heads up that you may experience some turbulence as you read this book.

Just as turbulence is often a part of riding on an airplane, reading a book that challenges your thinking and beliefs may cause some slight turbulence. If any discomfort is experienced, please don't abort the trip because of a brief bit of discomfort you may encounter. If you abort your journey because of a little turbulence on the way, what would you miss out on?

This book has something for every reader, and it is my prayer that it will serve to advise, prepare, inform, educate and encourage you. I'm certain there may be things you learn for the first time as well as things you may have already learned the hard way through your own personal experiences. Come along this journey with me and when you finish this book, I assure you it will have been worth the investment of not only your resources, but also your time. So, thank you for taking this journey with me. It's going to be a great trip!

LIFE LESSON ONE

Practical Economics: The Math We Need to Prosper

"Go to school. Get good grades, so you can get a good job" was all I heard from my mom and teachers when I was in school. I grew up in a small, farm town in Louisiana in a single parent household and my mom didn't have a high school education. She worked hard at low paying, domestic labor type jobs, as those were the only jobs available at the time for her. As far as she knew, getting good grades in school was the only pathway that would lead to getting ahead in life and as a result, she reminded me of this fact frequently. So, if my understanding was correct, the interpretation I should have walked away with after all those years of her "get a good education" reminders was the idea that my siblings and I should obtain good grades so we could secure good jobs that would pay us good money and enable us to enjoy good lives. With that engrained in my mind, I went to school and was an honor roll student all the way up until the 5th grade.

Back then, I didn't know what being rich looked like, outside of what I saw on television. However, I knew enough to know that we were poor even amongst other poor people. I knew I wanted something better out of life and being successful in school was the promised pathway to a better life.

You see, the educational system back then focused on teaching you how to earn money as an employee, usually through hard labor. This paradigm had a lot of validity during the time when factory work was booming, and blue-collar skilled laborers were in high demand. These types of jobs required very little creativity, critical thinking skills, or complex collaboration with others. Factory work simply required you to perform routine work, and you did exactly as you were told. You had one primary job to do and that's what you got paid for. No more, no less. If you were lucky to stay at the job long enough, you would receive a pension (monthly income from an investment account that you or the employer contributed to during your working years) once you retired.

There's nothing inherently wrong with the belief that going to school and making good grades will enable you to get a good job and earn a decent living. Putting forth effort to learn in school and being a productive employee does pay off. For many it did just that. Our efforts equipped us to earn enough income from our jobs to survive and live a modest life.

One critical component the school system failed to teach us was how to keep the money we earned and more importantly how to grow the money after we earned it using some form of investing. This lack of knowledge has been detrimental to the economic advancement of many people, including myself. I knew how to earn money by working hard and long hours, but I didn't learn how to keep the money, invest the money or grow the money until well into my adult years.

Throughout the last century, the ways in which people can earn money have evolved greatly due to the advancements of the internet, technology, e-commerce, social media, transportation and many other emerging industries. And as a result, many people, including myself, have enjoyed exponential financial growth.

There are more self-made millionaires now than any other time in history. There are also more college graduates now than any other point in history. Each year schools pump out graduates who, despite all the education and knowledge available to them, know very little about the skill of building wealth for themselves as individuals. Students are still being unconsciously taught how to build the wealth of others through their labor based on the premise of "go to school, get good grades, so you can get a good job." Our school system is still operating from the old paradigm of preparing laborers for a workforce that doesn't really exist anymore.

Therefore, the abundant accumulation of wealth promised to those who obtained good grades appears to be a reality for some, but only a mirage for most. A small minority of people are enjoying the vast majority of the wealth. For others, building wealth may never be obtained. With all of the access to knowledge and information at our fingertips, I'm puzzled by the fact that many people have not figured out how to win the game of life when it comes to their economics. But wait. That's one of the primary goals of obtaining an education, right? So, what are we missing? The answer is that many of us have simply been UNDER-EDUCATED when it comes to building wealth.

So where do we start? That's a great question. Let's talk about it.

The Eighth Wonder of the World

One of the reasons I suspect the wealth gap is expanding is because the wealthy have a more advanced mindset about money and finances than the basic math we were taught in school. I will address some of the differences in financial mindsets between the wealthy, middle class, and the poor in this book. However, if you'd like to learn more about these differences, please read my first book ***Unlock Your Mind...Unlock Your Money,*** which is available on Amazon.

In school, we were taught basic math (i.e., addition, subtraction, and division) and perhaps even took a class or two of advanced math (i.e., calculus, geometry, and trigonometry). However, many who went on to become wealthy learned a math concept that was not taught in school, or at least it wasn't taught when I was in school: ***compound interest***. Albert Einstein described compound interest as *"the eighth wonder of the world. He who understands it, earns it; he who doesn't, pays it."*

Wealthy people tend to be strategic and systematic savers and investors who capitalize on the principle of compound interest. Most others, on the other hand, have been unconsciously conditioned to be consumers. Investors make a profit from compound interest, while consumers are penalized by compound interest through consumer debt that results in higher payments, extended loan terms, etc. Investors learned the importance of growing and replicating their earned income from a job through investing. They learned the magic effect compound interest could have on their investments. Let's talk a bit more about the specifics of compound interest.

To compound something means to stack on top of or add to what's already there. Imagine a snowball rolling down a hill. As the snowball rolls down the hill, it picks up more and more snow. Similarly, compound interest describes the growth of one's initial financial investment (i.e., the principal) by the constant accrual of interest. Now the question is, what is interest? Interest in simple language is money earned solely from other money. So, it's your money growing more money. It's like you invested some money and your money had a baby and kept on having babies as long as your money remained invested in the account. Or imagine if you planted an apple seed, and the seed eventually became a tree that produced more and more apples each year. That's the magic of compound interest. The initial investment continues to produce more of itself.

For example, if you invest $1000 with an annual compound interest rate of 10%, after one year your $1000 investment will have earned $100 in interest. So, after one year your initial investment of $1000 will be worth $1100. If you didn't deposit any other money to the investment, after 20 years of compound interest being added at 10% a year, that $1000 investment will be worth $6728.00. Not bad, huh?

Now let's have some fun. If you invested $100,000 using the exact same formula of 10% compound interest earned annually over a 20-year period, it would be worth $672,750. Now, do you see why compound interest is so powerful? Your money had babies and then the babies had babies. Now you have "money grand babies," – and a whole bunch of them at that.

Let's say you put away $833.33 a month or $192.30 a week starting at the age of 20. In one year, you would have saved $10,000.00 ($9,999.60 to be exact). If you saved $10,000.00 a year for ten years, by the age of 30, you would have $100,000.00. If you simply invested that $100,000.00 with an annual compound interest rate of 10% for the next 20 years without adding any additional money, by the time you reach the age of 50 years old, you could have earned the $672,750 mentioned earlier. Wealthy people have a mindset of investing and are willing to exercise delayed gratification by investing the money they earn now to start building wealth for the future. Wealthy people are not afraid to invest some of their earned money to educate themselves on how to make their money earn money. They attend seminars, workshops, hire financial coaches or advisors, and read books frequently about money. The question I'm asking you and that you must ask yourself is "Are you willing to sacrifice some of the comforts you spend your money on now in order to take advantage of compound interest and start building your wealth?"

You may be asking yourself, where can I earn 10% compound interest? One of the safest investment tools used by investors are Mutual Funds and Index Funds. These funds offer a great deal of diversity as they consist of several publicly traded companies under one "fund" or umbrella that tries to match the stock market earnings. In essence instead of owning individual stocks in one company, these funds allow you to own a small piece of hundreds of different companies' stocks. Mutual funds and index funds historically earn 10 percent or more in compound interest over a 20-year time period. Seek out a financial advisor to help you get started.

Many people are simply unaware of compound interest and the power it has as a wealth building tool. Like myself, we were under-educated. I wish someone would've explained compound interest to me when I was younger. I wasted so much money in my young adult life buying name brand tennis shoes, clothing, and jewelry. And what's worse, I bought used luxury cars with high mileage on them only to end up spending more money repairing the car than what I actually paid for the car itself. It's embarrassing to admit some of the dumb things I did with money. Looking back, I can admit I was more concerned about "looking" like I had money and collecting cool points than I was about actually "having" money and growing it. I was more concerned about buying the Nike shoes instead of buying the Nike stock. I never had nice things growing up, so I spent a lot of money on nice things to impress other people and make me feel better about myself. I had a low self-image, low self-esteem, and I used the money I made to camouflage it. Sometimes I ask myself if I would've made the sacrifices if I had known about compound interest. I can't really say, but I'd like to think I would have. I'm a numbers guy and once I'm exposed to the numbers, I generally align my behaviors to match.

If you're reading this book and you're under the age of 20, this information, if you apply it, can make you a millionaire over the next 20-40 years. Hey, what's the worst that can happen if you take advantage of compound interest? Maybe your sacrifices now only lead to you becoming a hundred thousand-aire instead of a millionaire. From my perspective, that's not such a bad problem to have. I assure you, whatever you save and invest will be worth more than the name brand tennis shoes, clothes, or electronics that you would spend money on today.

If you want to see how compound interest works and you want to play with some numbers, you can easily find investment calculators online that will allow you to insert the amount you want to invest, how often you want to invest, the interest rate, etc., and see for yourself how easy it is to become wealthy with the right knowledge, discipline, and willingness to sacrifice short-term comfort for long-term enjoyment. I highly encourage you to invest some time into learning how money works. After all, no one else is going to do it for you because no one else cares more about your money than you.

I hope you are now able to see how the mathematical principle of compound interest is applicable to your financial life. Learning this one piece of mathematical information might have been more helpful for our financial life than learning how to solve for X in algebraic equations – wouldn't you agree? Unless you're going into a field to become a chemist, engineer, statistician or enter some other specialized field of work, the many years of algebra, calculus, etc. could have been supplemented with more practical financial knowledge that people have to deal with in everyday life. The magic of compound interest and investing is critical to your financial wellbeing and I hope you are able to take advantage of this tool moving forward. Now let's shift our attention to another important number that wasn't taught in school: the credit score.

Understanding Your Credit Report and Score

Your Credit Report: What is it and how does it work?

As a financial coach, I've found that most people don't think about the impact of credit until it's too late and the damage has been done. As I think back on my experience, I don't recall learning about credit until I was 19 years old and had joined the U.S. Navy after graduating from high school. Prior to then, I had no real concept of what credit was or why it was even important. My parents didn't talk about credit. My mom had bad credit and my dad paid cash for everything, so he had no credit. And school certainly didn't teach me about this critical piece of knowledge. Most of my exposure to credit came from hearing adults talk about how bad their credit was. They never told me why it was bad or how it got bad. It was just bad. I did have a close family member try to teach me about credit once. She said "You gotta have good credit to buy stuff and the way you get good credit is to apply for small loans and pay them back the minimum payments monthly. This will make your credit score go up." That was my first real introduction to credit. Other than that, I was left to figure the rest out on my own.

At 19 years old, I was stationed at the Navy base in Jacksonville, Florida and was technically "grown" or an adult. The only problem was, I knew very little about money or credit, which are key components of survival as an adult. By this point in my life, I had successfully matriculated though 13 years of K-12 education (yes, I had a bonus year for being stupid and not prioritizing my grades, so I had the opportunity to do 5th grade twice). I had successfully completed military bootcamp and A school, which is military specialty training school to learn my craft for the military. I still, however, had no clue about how to navigate real life financial matters like credit, credit scores, credit reports, debt, saving money, investing, etc. I was young and well...dumb!

Of course, as most 19 year–old's, my top concern was not my financial future. I had one dominant thought at that phase of my life. I desperately needed a car. But I didn't have any money saved and my parents didn't have any money to help me. I was miles away from my family, I didn't have many friends at the time, and the few new friends I did have were just as broke as I was and had no cars. So, I had to endure many weekends stuck on the Navy base with no personal transportation. If I wanted to leave the base, I had to ride in a shuttle that would take us to the mall and back, and I had to wait for it to pick me up. I thought to myself, "How am I going to ever get a girl with no transportation?" I needed my own car stat!

My job didn't pay enough money for me to buy a brand-new car, and I didn't have any money saved to buy a car with cash. And here's where my family member's advice about credit came back to my memory. I needed to establish some credit so I could get a loan from the bank to help me buy a car. Yep, that's exactly what I need to do. So off I went to the jewelry store in the mall where I applied for a store credit card and was instantly approved for a $300 line of credit. This was the first financial decision I'd made as an adult. I remember purchasing a gold Seiko watch for $280.00. Most of my other watches all cost under $10.00 making this the most expensive watch I'd ever purchased. This new watch looked really good, too. It made me feel like I imagined rich people felt every day, and I couldn't wait to show it off. It was my version of a Rolex and boy was I proud. I was happy about the watch, but even happier that I had started the journey into adulthood with my first financial purchase. Establishing my first line of credit was step one. At the time, I didn't realize I was embarking on a credit card journey that would lead to me becoming entangled with debt for years to come. We'll talk more about this later. At that moment, I had tasted the exhilarating feeling that comes with the magical words "YOU'RE APPROVED" and let me tell you, I was hooked!

Continuing with the advice I received about building credit; I opened multiple other accounts in order to build and establish a credit history. Eventually, I was approved to borrow $5000 from Navy Federal Credit Union to buy a used silver Volvo 740 from my cousin. Wow! This credit stuff was magical. I could buy stuff now and pay for it later. It solved my need for a car and helped me establish a credit history. I was doing life well. Or so I thought.

The type of loan I was able to get for the car is what bankers refer to as a "secured line of credit" which essentially means the lender has the money they loan you secured by the item you purchase (house, car, etc.). If you don't pay them back, they take possession of the asset (car, house, etc.) which they loaned you money for. If you happen to know someone who's had a vehicle repossessed or a home foreclosed on, that's what happened. Since I had my paycheck going directly to the credit union from the Navy, they gladly loaned me the money. Plus, the title to the car was in their name – so it was an easy decision for them, as the bank had little risk. Banks make money by loaning out money and earning interest on the money over the amount of time it takes you to pay the loan back. Essentially, the bank is benefitting off the compound interest principle I discussed earlier.

I was gleefully and unknowingly on my way into credit card bondage. I made all my payments on time and within a few months, I ascended into the "good" credit score heavens. "So, this is what having a good credit score feels like," I thought. I felt like passengers riding in first class on airplanes. My nose was slightly tilted in an upward position. I felt rich and powerful as if I could buy whatever I wanted...on credit at least.

From the moment I obtained my first credit card in 1999 until 2006, I built my financial life around having good credit and maintaining a high credit score.

I was addicted. My addiction to having "good credit" was so bad at times, I remember if my scores went down because I paid off something, I would literally go borrow more money for something else that I really didn't need just to increase my scores again. I was obsessed with maintaining a high credit score because to me, at the time, having good credit carried greater value than having money. And since I didn't have any money saved, credit was my money. As you continue reading, you'll learn more about how I navigated my way through this overwhelming and seemingly impossible challenge to overcome untangling myself from credit card debt.

So, what is a credit score?

Before we go any further into this discussion of credit let's get the basics out of the way. The origin of the word credit came from the middle French "cre'dit" which meant "belief or trust." So, inherent in the word credit, a certain level of trust is involved. We'll talk more about this later. The credit scoring system is known as the FICO score. FICO is short for Fair Isaac Corporation. The Fair Isaac Corporation is a private company/corporation that collects personal data on individuals' spending habits and payment history to determine their credit worthiness. The founders, Bill Fair and Earl Isaac initially created this mathematical formula in 1956 to help banks determine if they were willing to lend money to individuals based on the probability of those individuals paying it back given their payment history and credibility. It later evolved into what we now know as a primary source that lenders, employers, landlords and others use to make predictive decisions about the likelihood an individual would make timely payments for goods and services purchased.

How does the Credit Score work?

A credit score is somewhat like a school report card. It's a numerical indicator used to show how well you are managing your personal financial affairs. In our society now, it is nearly impossible to live without some form of credit. The word credit as we generally use it today is a nicer, interchangeable word for debt. The debt balances you accumulate on credit are reported to three credit bureaus on a monthly basis. There are three major credit bureaus that collect data from lending institutions about you and your patterns of paying back your debts: Transunion, Experian, and Equifax.

The three bureaus use a mathematical algorithm/formula that takes into account information provided by institutions that have loaned you money or provided a good or service to you, including your existing payment history, amount of debt you currently owe, how long you have been making payments and your loan balances to determine if you are creditworthy. The mathematical algorithm used by the bureaus then generates a number that is called your "credit score." Whenever you request a loan in the future, a loan officer reviews the information from your credit report and your current credit score to decide whether or not to approve or deny you for the loan you requested.

In essence, your credit score lets potential lenders know what type of borrower you will likely be. Your credit score can range from 300-850. The higher your score is, the better. A credit score ranging between 300-579 is considered poor. 580-669 is considered fair. 670-740 is considered good. 740-799 is considered very good. Anything over 800 is considered excellent.

What is your Credit Report?

Your credit report is a detailed document that has all of your basic financial information on it, not including the amount of money you have in your bank accounts. The credit report has the balance of what you currently owe. For example, if you financed a vehicle and you still owe $17,000.00 on it, the credit report will show that you owe $17,000.00 to the lender you borrowed the money from. It will also show how much your monthly payments are. This information is then used by lenders to determine your debt-to-income ratio, which we'll talk about later.

Additionally, your credit report includes your complete name, date of birth, social security number and any alias/other names you may have used in the past. It will also have your current address along with any previous addresses where you've resided. It will show any loans that you've ever taken out from a lending institution and how you repaid the loans. It has every lending institution you've ever borrowed money from and whether or not you repaid them in a timely manner. In a nutshell, the credit report is a collection of data analyzing your payment behavior based on previous loans. Lenders, employers, landlords, and others use your credit report and credit score to make decisions about you. They use this to try to determine your character. The higher your credit score is, the easier it will be to get a loan and the better your interest rates will be on the financing. Landlords will choose you to rent their property to over someone with a lower credit score.

Why is all of this important?

Most lenders in America use this system to determine if you are a high, medium or low risk borrower. If you want to receive favorable outcomes with better terms and lower interest rates for loans, you must maintain a "good credit score". While I have concerns about the use of credit given my experiences with credit during my early years, I believe it is important that everyone learn how to play the credit game in order to win.

So how do I establish credit?

The only way to establish credit is to borrow money. Borrowing money from a business or lending institution to pay for a product or service is referred to as *financing*. Essentially financing is when you get the product or service without paying for it outright with cash. Instead of paying for the product or service up front with cash, you borrow the money for it (finance it) and then pay for the goods or services over time in monthly installments with terms ranging from 12 months to 30 years. The business entity still gets the full payment for the product or service while capitalizing on the principle of compound interest depending on how long you take to pay the balance off.

For example, if you go to a car dealer and they allow you to drive off in a vehicle that you didn't pay cash for, the dealership or a bank "financed" the loan for you. As far as the dealer is concerned, they got their money upfront. You are then expected to repay the loan according to the terms you and the dealer/lender agreed to on a monthly basis. As you make your payments on time, the lender reports your payment history to the credit bureau on a monthly basis. Over time, you have built a history and based on your payment history, this will establish your credit. If you make your payments on time, this works in your favor. If you don't make your payments on time or you are late making your payments, this hurts you by lowering your credit score.

Keep your word. *(Some readers may experience slight turbulence...fasten your seatbelts)*
Your credit score is about credibility. How credible are you? If you say you're going to do something, can people count on you to do it in the timeframe you said you would do it? Credibility is not only important when it comes to money. It's also important when it comes to other things that have nothing to do with money. The reason people have bad credit is because they didn't keep their word on a prior loan or agreement. Let's say you borrow $100 from a family member or friend and promise to pay them back within a month. A month comes and goes, and you have not paid the loan back. Several months go by and you not only haven't paid back the loan, but you haven't even communicated with them about plans to repay the loan. This type of behavior damages your credibility. The person who loaned you money may not ever say anything else to you about it, but in their mind, your credibility is trash. They will likely never loan you money again. Why? Because you didn't keep your word. They can't trust you. This pattern of not paying back what you borrow causes lenders to deny loaning you money. Based on your past behavior, they can't trust you. Creating trust issues means you will be penalized by lenders. Those penalties come in the form of charging you higher interest rates to borrow money because you are considered high risk. Given the high cost of poor credibility, I encourage you to make your payments on time and keep your debt balances low.

What lowers your credit score?

- **Making payments late**. Late payments on credit cards, auto loans and student loans can have a two-to-three-month impact on your score. Making a late payment past 30 days on your home mortgage can have a huge effect on your score. In fact, it can take an entire year for your credit score to rebound from making a single late mortgage payment.
- **Applying for multiple credit accounts at once**. Applying for multiple credit cards at one time suggests you're in trouble financially and you're looking for a quick fix to get you out. Applying for several consumer credit cards and department store cards in a short period of

time tells lenders that you are financially unstable and living above your means.

- **Allowing accounts to go into collections.** When you do not repay the money you've borrowed to pay for goods and services, the lender will call you repeatedly for a period of time to collect payment. This also applies to service providers (utility companies, cell phone carriers, cable companies, etc.). If the lender is unable to collect payment from you after multiple attempts, they will likely sell the loan balance to a collection agency for a reduced amount of what is owed. For example, if a person owes $1000 in medical bills and does not pay it, the hospital may sell the balance to a collection agency for $100. A collection agency is a private company that buys bad debt and attempts to collect the unpaid balance. The collection agency will report the unpaid debt to your credit report as a collection. This reporting will have a negative impact on your credit score. Collection agencies use this tactic to pressure individuals to repay what they have borrowed because of the negative impact it has on their credit score. Oftentimes, it works. If a collection agency can get you to repay $500 of the original $1000 balance, they still made a $400 profit. See how this works? They used the negativity of your credit score to convince you to repay the debt you created or are responsible for. Any bank considering loaning money to you will frown upon these negative accounts on your credit report because it shows that you are not credible when it comes to paying your debts.
- **Not having established credit.** If you don't have a track record of borrowing and repaying the money that is reported to the credit bureaus, you won't be able to establish a credit score. This doesn't mean you have bad credit. It means you have no credit. It is common for young adults just graduating from high school not to have credit. There are some individuals who have never had credit because they used cash for the majority of their purchases like my dad who I mentioned earlier.
- **Maxing out your credit cards.** Maxing out your credit card is another way to lower your credit score. For example, if you have a credit card with a maximum limit of $3000.00 and you have a balance of $2940.00,

lenders will consider you a high risk for a loan because a maxed-out credit card suggests you are living above your financial means. Because you are stretched out too far financially, you are a high risk for them, meaning you likely won't be able to repay the loan. To maintain a good credit score, you should keep your credit card usage low and pay the balance off completely each month if possible. Paying off the balance communicates that you are not a high-risk borrower and that you manage your money responsibly.

- **New credit**: It's important to note that opening a new line of credit may initially lower your credit score. Usually, your score will go back up to where it was prior to the new debt after two to three months. It may even increase slightly. Fortunately, the negative impact of a newly opened account is usually a short-term situation.
- **Debt to Income too high**: Debt to income ratio, also referred to by lenders as your (DTI) is what a mortgage lender uses to determine if the amount of total debt you have and the total income you have is too close. They take a percentage of what you earn in income and compare it to the total amount of debt payments you are responsible for. Most lenders generally like to see the debt to income around 43 percent or less. So, if you earn $4500 a month and your monthly debt obligations are $4200 a month, you are in grave financial danger in the eyes of a lender. Your debt obligations should be around $1935.00 a month. The more debt you have that's consuming your income, the higher risk you are to lenders and this will negatively impact your credit score.
- **Foreclosures:** If you do not make the monthly mortgage payments on your home, after six months of missing the payments, the lender will foreclose, or legally take possession of the home. A foreclosure will destroy your credit score. While going through a home foreclosure is not a life sentence, it usually takes a minimum of 3 years for you to recover and purchase another home. I went through a foreclosure, and it was not a pleasant experience. Like I said, you can recover from it, but it will sting for a while. Your score can easily drop 100-200 points as the result of a foreclosure. Few, if any, lenders will be willing to loan you

money with a recent foreclosure on your credit report. From the lender's perspective, your inability to maintain shelter for yourself means you will likely skip out on repaying them for something that's not as essential for your survival.

- **Evictions:** If you don't pay your rent for the month after 30 days, the landlord can file court documents to force you to move out of the residence for non-payment of rent. This, too, will have a negative impact on your credit score. An eviction says you signed an agreement to pay a certain amount of money for a certain number of months to a landlord, but you failed to keep your end of the agreement. Looking at it from a lender's perspective, your lack of priority in maintaining a roof over your head means you won't prioritize paying them back. If the lender decides to loan you money knowing your financial history, they will charge a significantly higher interest rate for the loan to ensure that they will be able to get most of their money back. When you try to find housing again, the new landlord or property manager will likely require you to pay a double deposit for rent because your credit history suggests you are a high risk for not paying. They do this to hedge their potential losses if you decide not to pay rent.
- **Repossessions:** If you finance automobiles, furniture, appliances, etc., and don't make the monthly payments, the owner of the items can take the items back because of non-payment and report this to the credit bureaus. This is called repossession. Others considering loaning you money for future items like a car, furniture, etc. will not take kindly to seeing a repossession on your credit report. Why? Because a repossession says to them you can't be trusted. There's that word again. You borrowed something and agreed to repay a set amount on a set date, and you broke the agreement. You did not keep your word.
- **Bankruptcy:** Bankruptcy was designed to serve as a legal loophole for major corporations to evade paying back significant amounts of debt they accumulated but could not afford to pay back. Unfortunately, it has become common practice for individuals to file for bankruptcy for small amounts of debt they can't pay back. Filing for bankruptcy will absolutely destroy your credit and other aspects of your financial life.

Depending on the type of bankruptcy you file, bankruptcy can stay on your credit for 7-10 years and it will be a negative stain on your financial life. Bankruptcy can make it extremely difficult to obtain financing for vehicles, homes, or any other loans/lines of credit. Bankruptcy tells lenders you will take the easy way out when you get into a financial jam instead of paying what is owed. Bankruptcy protects you legally from the liability, but it destroys your credit in the process. Corporations form Limited Liability Corporations (LLC's) which provide them with legal protections that allow the registered "corporation" or "company" to file for bankruptcy without attaching the company's CEO or owner to the debt owed. However, when an individual files for bankruptcy, the bankruptcy is attached to the individual personally. To help you understand this better, imagine it's raining outside and two people are standing outside in the rain. One of them is standing under a canopy or large umbrella that protects them from the rain, while the other person has no protection from the rain at all. This is the difference between corporations filing bankruptcy and individuals filing bankruptcy. Both are standing in the rain, but only the individual without protection will get wet. Because of the implications and negative consequences of bankruptcy on the individual, I strongly discourage any individuals from filing bankruptcy. Bankruptcy as a strategy was not designed with individuals in mind. I understand it may feel like you are facing an insurmountable amount of debt and that bankruptcy is the only answer. As a financial coach, I've helped lots of people successfully get out of debt using a plan and discipline. Regaining control of a negative financial situation can usually be accomplished without filing bankruptcy. When I lost my first property to foreclosure, if I'd had the option of filing bankruptcy, I probably would have taken it. I was emotionally overwhelmed and anything that would have alleviated the pain in that dark moment of my life would have been something I would have agreed to. However, knowing what I now know, I'm glad no one presented that to me as an option.

- **Judgements:** Lenders have an option to send your past due debt to an attorney to file a lawsuit against you for payment. If the court agrees with the lender, you will have a judgment filed against you demanding repayment of the debt you owe. To ensure repayment of the debt, your bank accounts may be frozen, a lien (right to keep possession of property belonging to another person until a debt owed by the person is paid) may be put against your property, and your wages may be garnished (legally withheld) by your employer in order to pay off the debt. As a real estate broker, I've had multiple clients who earned high incomes but were unable to obtain a home loan because of a judgment on their credit report.

How can you increase your credit score?

- Make your payments on time. Set a weekly or monthly schedule to ensure you don't miss a payment. I teach clients to choose one day each week to pay bills. This way, each week you are making sure you don't miss a bill. You can also set up auto draft where the payment comes directly from your account. The day I chose is called "Money Monday's" and that's when all the bills that came in for the week are paid. These strategies will essentially guarantee you don't miss a payment that will negatively impact your credit score. The on-time payment history will increase your credit score.
- Keep your credit card account balances (how much you owe) below 25 percent of the maximum credit card limit (how much is available to borrow).
- Pay your debts off sooner than scheduled.
- Keep your debt-to-income ratio low.
- When possible, only use credit for large ticket items like homes, automobiles, etc.
- Dispute the accuracy of collection accounts on your credit report if they are listed twice. Many times, a collection agency will report a delinquent account at the same time the original debtor is reporting the same delinquent account. Having multiple collections for the same account makes it look like you have multiple negative accounts, which compounds the negative impact on your credit score.

Hopefully, you have a better understanding of the credit report, credit scores, and other things that impact you financially. Now let's address the other component that we were not taught in school. The "D" word. DEBT.

Debt...Is it a TOOL or a CURSE?

There are multiple types of debt one can experience. For the sake of simplicity, I will focus primarily on three areas of debt: consumer debt, mental debt and emotional debt.

Debt #1: Consumer Debt

The most common debt people are familiar with is what we call "consumer debt" or personal debt, which is money an individual borrows in exchange for goods or services that do not appreciate in value. Most often this type of debt is created when individuals don't have cash available to purchase something they need or desire. Instead of paying cash, they borrow money or use a credit card to purchase items on credit and then pay the money back over a period of time in installments. This consumer debt is most often utilized in the form of credit cards, department store cards, travel credit cards, etc. Items generally purchased using this method are small household items like televisions and appliances, or personal items like clothing, jewelry, vacations, entertainment, etc.

Many will argue that consumer debt is healthy for the economy – to which I reply, "Whose economy?" It's healthy for the ones profiting off your lack of available cash to purchase the things you need or want. Many retailers rely on consumer debt to stay in business, particularly when they sell products or services that are not essential for survival. When people can't pay full price for products or services they desire, they mentally justify spending money for non-essential products and services because they can pay for it in installments over time. When you finance items instead of paying for them up front in cash, you actually end up spending more money for the item when you factor in the interest you pay over time. This type of consumption is usually motivated and driven by our insatiable appetite for more and more things that are advertised on the myriad of platforms in society today. From television, radio, social media, billboards, vehicles, signs, friends, and emails, we are constantly bombarded with advertisements that appeal to our emotions and cause us to respond like a toddler in a grocery store check-out line screaming "I want it. I want it now!"

Because marketing companies have studied human behavior for years and they know we generally make spending decisions based largely on emotions and not intellect, they spend billions of dollars trying to figure out how to appeal to those emotions to get your dollars. One of the most frequent emotions they rely on is fear: fear of loss or missed opportunities. You undoubtedly have seen ads using phrases like "limited time only" or "hurry, this one won't last." This tactic is an effective strategy because it appeals to our emotions – in particular, fear of missing out – if we don't act fast to secure whatever they are selling.

I have no issue with a great marketing campaign, salesperson or advertisements for that matter. Sales help the world function. My issue, however, is when people are influenced to depart from their hard-earned money for the sake of "stuffitis" – a term coined to describe people's tendency to buy more and more stuff simply for the sake of buying it and then living the majority of their lives working to pay for it.

Where did the notion of consumer debt come from?

This type of consumer debt, believe it or not, has not been a way of life for hundreds of years. As a matter of fact, it's a little over 70 years old. It is believed that this type of debt consumption was not by design, but more of an unintentional discovery. Some historians suggest this strategy was initially created by a German psychologist who studied human behaviors and believed he could influence people's behavior when it came to voting. His theory proved to be correct and the concept of appealing directly to the human emotions of desiring a better life and promising to make that life accessible to the masses helped his candidate win the election. His strategy was so effective, it became the model for voting as we know it.

The idea that originated to help a politician win an election, suddenly turned its attention to capitalism. Someone had the bright idea that maybe we can sell more cars, homes, radios, appliances, etc., if we appeal to people's emotions and advertise products directly to them. And so it began, commercials started featuring attractive people showcasing products from cars to cigarettes to vacuum cleaners in order to sell more of their goods. It worked! Before you knew it, everyone wanted the items they heard about on the radio or seen on television, billboards, and signs in their neighbor's yard. This might be where the phrase "keeping up with the Joneses" came from.

With such a growing demand for goods, a political economic recovery plan after the great depression where then President Franklin Roosevelt promised a brighter future for all, came this model of consumption as we know it today. As the economy began to recover, appetites and hunger for more stuff began to grow. The only problem was people didn't have the actual money to keep up with their appetites.

This is where credit came in as an alternate way to purchase things for those who didn't have the cash available. Bankers and businesses figured out how to meet the demands of consumption by becoming financiers. Loaning money directly to consumers became big business. They started loaning consumers money to buy things and accepting repayment of the loan with "interest" over time. It became a very profitable business model, and it still is today.

Prior to the use of credit-based purchasing options, people were forced to live based upon delayed gratification. They purchased items in cash, which meant they had to save and wait to purchase things they needed and wanted. In instances when people wanted to purchase something but could not pay the full amount up front, retail stores offered the option to hold the items in stock or "lay them away" by making a small cash deposit and then paying off the remaining balance over time. Once they paid off the balance, then and only then could they retrieve the items. Remember the school clothes my mom bought me every year? Well, they were all bought on "lay-away."

Unfortunately, the introduction of credit-based financing opened the floodgates to hyper-consumption. Because people no longer had to wait to purchase items in full before they took them home, people began buying more and more things knowing they could pay for them later.

By this point of the book, I hope you're able to see that you as the consumer are being penalized for borrowing money on credit – whether you are borrowing from banks or retail stores.

I remember going to the bank with my mom as a child and they would always have those little "dum dum" suckers in a cup to give out to the kids. I thought it was cool that the banks cared about the kids and wanted us to have some candy. Now that I'm older and I have devoted my life to learning about finances, I see things a bit differently. I realize now that those suckers were symbolism. Get it? We were the "dum dum" suckers being ushered into debt so the bank could make money off us paying them interest for the loans they provided.

While consuming goods using credit cards is a fairly mainstream practice, it wasn't always this way. The first credit card, called a diners club card, was created by a restaurant back in 1950. Then Bank of America started mailing unsolicited pre-approved credit cards called "BankAmericard Visa" to households in 1958. Years later, Sears, Roebuck and Company department stores created their own credit card to provide in-house financing, meaning Sears would finance the items themselves instead of sending consumers to the banks. This became a large part of their business model. Because of the initial success of credit card use for increasing sales and generating additional profit from interest, other entities soon followed suit giving birth to modern-day credit cards like Visa, MasterCard and American Express. Retail stores, car dealerships, colleges and others learned how to sell more products using credit and they profited billions of dollars from it.

While banks and credit card companies profited significantly from the interest paid by consumers, consumers did not fare so well. The amount of consumer debt the average person carries is alarming. The average interest rate on a credit card is 18 – 24 percent compounded monthly, which means the person sinks deeper into debt at a rapid rate. The statistics vary from year to year, but on average, people carry between $6000 – $8000 in credit card consumer debt. This is not including payments for cars, student loans, rent/mortgages, and other basic necessities of life. As a financial coach, I've encountered many young adults who feel trapped by debt during the early years of their journey into adulthood. Many are depressed and feel like a failure due to the excessive amounts of debt they have accumulated that consequently choke the life out of their economics.

I know what some of you may be thinking, so let me go ahead and address it. Yes, it is possible for consumers to use credit cards to their benefit, but it requires a significant amount of discipline and doesn't factor in risk. Therefore,

I do not encourage using credit cards. However, if you follow the advice I gave earlier on paying off the entire balance when the credit card statement arrives and only use a credit card if you know you have the means to repay the balance off every month, you will have a better chance of not getting burned by credit cards and consumer debt. The key is to control your appetites that compel you to purchase things on credit that are not assets or necessities.

If you currently use credit cards for your purchases, be mindful that the banks and credit card companies make their profit from the interest you pay. If you only pay the required minimum payment without paying the balance off on the credit card, you end up paying more than the actual cost of the item when you factor in interest that profits the lender but costs you. Of course, lenders will not encourage you to pay the entire balance off because that's not profitable for them.

To understand the impact of interest on consumer debt, let's look at an example. Let's say you purchase a refrigerator from a department store for $1000.000. Your minimum monthly payment is only $30.00 (usually 3% of the balance) a month with a 20% interest rate. It will take 50 months to pay off the balance and you will have given the credit card company $472.00 in interest in addition to the original $1000 you borrowed. So, in essence your refrigerator cost you $1472.00. If you just like giving away your money, send me a text and I will send you my cashapp so you can make a contribution to my dreams of owning an Island and naming it "Lovenia."

Seriously though, if you are going to use a credit card, please do your best to pay the balance off quickly to avoid paying all the extra money in interest. Banks may not like me giving you this advice, but I'm not concerned about them. I'm looking out for the people who were under-educated like me and didn't know how much of their fortune they were giving away to banks because of lack of awareness.

Consumer debt can be very destructive and has caused many families to break up due to the stress that financial strain and debt can place on a marriage. Data show that one of the leading causes of suicide among young people is financial stress and feelings of hopelessness. Small businesses have closed because they took on debt to open the business but the profits made were not sufficient to sustain the business or pay the debt off. Family and friends have fallen out with one another because of borrowed money. There's a scripture in the bible that warned us in Proverbs 22:7 which says, "The rich rule/govern over the poor, and the borrower is slave to the lender." The end result is the credit card and financing companies are getting richer and the consumers are getting poorer.

By reading this section, I hope you are able to examine the risks, rewards, and come up with a plan that works best for you and your financial situation.

Debt #2: Mental Debt

Now this next debt is what I like to call "mental debt." Mental debt refers to a perceived obligation to adhere to or meet certain standards or oblige the requests of others according to others' expectations. Many times, these expectations are not directly handed down to us, but they are suggested, implied or encouraged by the culture. There's an unspoken rule that you are obligated to meet the expectations of parents, relatives, co-workers, friends, or even organizations for that matter. When we don't meet those expectations, there are subtle – or perhaps not so subtle – consequences that negatively impact us.

For example, in street culture, if you know that one of your friends did something illegal, there's an expectation that you do not tell the authorities, even if not telling the authorities means you could potentially suffer a negative consequence or punishment. Even in instances when you, as an innocent person are blamed for the crime your friend committed, there's still an expectation that you don't tell the authorities that your friend committed the crime. This expectation not to disclose problematic behavior exists in many aspects of life. In urban street culture, when you tell on someone it's called being a "snitch." In the suburbs they call it being a "tattle tell." In corporate settings it's called being a "whistleblower." There's even a phrase, "snitches get stitches," that implies that anyone who tells on a guilty party will be injured or experience negative consequences as a result of their failure or refusal to keep quiet about what they know. While mental debt is not the same as literal financial debt, it can be just as much of a burden to carry as any other debt. Oftentimes, when I ask people which debt they think is worse, the overwhelming majority say the mental debt is worse. Many people are existing with this burden of mental debt, but very few are talking about it.

Any time someone has an expectation of you, it can be viewed as a debt. Whether you agree to comply with the expectation or not, it's still a debt if there's an expectation that you do something to please someone else. Within the concept of mental debt is a sense of entitlement wherein people believe something is owed to them that they did not necessarily earn. In mental debt, people are expected to comply with another person's expectation of them even if doing so would cause them to compromise some aspect of their lives.

Here's an example. When a guy takes a lady out to dinner for a date, there's ALWAYS an expectation. The guy likely has an expectation of developing a relationship with the lady over time that may lead to a sexual relationship at some point or even marriage. The guy may be holding an expectation that if he takes the woman out, has a good time and pays for dinner, he will be rewarded in some capacity. Now I know what you're thinking...not all guys think like that. Bull crap! While admittedly, not all guys think about sex immediately, often times they have some type of expectation. It's the expectation of a reward that motivated him to ask for the date in the first place.

The same goes for women. Using the same dating scenario, the woman may have an expectation that the man pays for dinner. Why? Because that's the script given to us by culture. It may not be a spoken expectation by the man or woman, but trust me when I say that both of them have expectations, even if they deny those expectations in the beginning. I recognize that this may be hard to hear, and it may even be the cause of turbulence when it comes to your perspective on dating. As the pilot, I encourage you to ride through the storm on this one and take heed to my words. You will have a much better chance of landing at your relationship destiny if you keep in mind the mental debt often involved in dating relationships.

As I close out this section, I would like to offer you a way to test out how mental debt works in your life. When you have expectations of people and they don't meet your expectations, do you become disappointed, angry, sad, resentful or revengeful? If you said yes to any of those emotional reactions, then you likely hold people to mental debt. And what makes it a mental debt you ask? The fact that you ***felt*** like you were owed something whether you actually were or not. Another way to determine if mental debt is present in your life is to think about an instance when you were invited to attend someone's party, and you didn't want to go, but you went anyway. What made you go? If you went primarily to avoid negative feelings such as guilt about disappointing the person by not going, you were operating from a place of mental debt. Mental debt can range from mild to extreme. And, at times can feel like bondage as in the case of consumer debt. In order to improve our quality of life and sense of peace, we need to monitor the level of mental debt we place on others as well as the debt others place on us. When we carry a huge load of mental debt, it can negatively impact our physical and psychological well-being.

Debt #3: Emotional Debt

Third on the list is emotional debt, which is ladened with guilt and obligatory demands that you may not necessarily agree with. Or perhaps it's the feeling of being indebted to someone because they did something for you, and you have become an indentured servant of theirs for eternity. On the surface, emotional debt can look like mental debt, but there's a slight difference between the two. Mental debt occurs when you are somewhat unaware of all the unspoken expectations of others or when something is just culturally expected of you. Emotional debt is different because you are aware of the expectations of others, but the difference is you may not want to meet those expectations.

Sometimes this debt can come from parents. For example, many children were strongly encouraged to follow a certain career path, attend a certain school, or pledge a certain fraternity/sorority because their parents did. Some people are teaching school now, not because they have a passion to educate and empower the next generation, but because their mother was a teacher and that's what was expected of them. Some preachers are pastoring churches because their father was a pastor. They don't necessarily feel a calling or desire to do it, but it's the expectation. Others may become policemen, firemen, doctors, etc. because their parents established an expectation of them and they feel obligated to meet those expectations. What's worse, some people dislike other people strictly because their parents taught them to.

Another example of emotional debt is when people have helped you in the past and they feel as if you are now obligated to them for the rest of your life. They make statements like "if it wasn't for me..." or "you wouldn't be nothing without me." One of my favorites is "remember when I..." These statements can weigh you down emotionally if you aren't careful. Usually, the people who are closest to us are the ones who wield this type of debt. Because we are close to them and we care about them on a personal level, their expectations really impact us emotionally. Our care and love for them compels us to succumb to their expectations. I encourage you not to allow the tactic of emotional debt to control you or get you down. You have the freedom to say yes, and you have the freedom to say no. Do not allow people to manipulate you. Set some boundaries and learn to say no.

Trust me, I get it. Saying no can be painful because of the emotions involved; however, saying no is an absolute necessity. The way I see it, you have two types of pain to choose from. You can choose the long-term pain of being indebted to and manipulated by others, or you can choose the short-term pain that comes with saying no in order to avoid the long-term pain of emotional debt. My friend, you cannot afford to carry emotional debt with you for the rest of your life. It's expensive and totally unsustainable.

As I conclude this section, I invite you to take inventory of the types of debt you're currently carrying. None of the three types of debt I discussed are healthy for us, and they can have devastating lifetime consequences. The stress induced by literal debt nearly killed me physically. Mental debt had me living beneath my full potential. And emotional debt nearly took me out spiritually and relationally with many people. I'm happy to announce to you that I have officially divorced all three of these debts and decided not to live with them anymore. Now that I'm free, I will do everything in my power to steer clear of these debts in the future. If you have experienced any of these debts, or are in debt now, I pray you are able to find freedom from this bondage. Prayerfully, as you were reading about the different types of debt, you saw yourself and were empowered to change the situation.

Now that you've learned how different types of debt can put you in the hole, let's talk about ways to climb out of the hole as well as minimize falling into the hole in the future. Come on over and let's talk about it.

Saving Money: The foundation for wealth building.

You don't have to be an architect to know that if you plan on building anything that will last and be sustained, it must have a solid and strong foundation. In similar fashion, wealth building requires a solid and strong foundation. The first step to building wealth is to develop a basic savings plan or strategy so you have something to build on in the future.

During seminars, podcasts, and private financial coaching sessions, I teach that the very first financial decision you need to make is to prioritize saving money. Just for a moment, let's take a quick trip back down memory lane. Try to think back on some of the financial advice or lessons you were taught by your parents or mentors growing up, maybe even write them down now so you can reference them later as you decide which areas you want to change and which areas, you'd like to stay the same when it comes to your finances.

For me personally, my journey to financial literacy was off to a slow start when I was growing up. I was told that I needed to save money, but I never saw it in practice. In fact, the people I looked up to were much better at spending money than they were at saving money. As the saying goes, more is caught than taught. Since I did not have a model of what saving looked like, I would hustle as a teenager to earn money, but I never figured out how to save any of it. Looking back as I reflect on my childhood memories now, I realize that part of the challenge with my mom saving money was that we often didn't have enough money to cover the basic essentials of life. Consequently, there was never anything to save because we were always at a deficit.

Fast forward to adulthood during my time in the Navy, I made more money than I had ever made in my life. Plus, I had no real expenses outside of a cell phone bill and car payment, as most of my living expenses were covered by the Navy. I lived on the ship rent free, and I ate free food on the base. With this set up, you'd think I would've been able to save a ton of money, right? But did I? Absolutely not. After my third year on the ship, I had received several promotions and I was earning even more money. However, when I left to go to my next military assignment in Dallas, TX, I believe I had a total of $800 saved. A measly $800 saved out of several thousand that I had possession of at one point in time.

You may be wondering how I could make a lot of money (especially since my expenses were low) and not have much money saved. It's simple. Saving money wasn't a priority for me. In my mind, I didn't have to save because I had another check coming from my job in two weeks. This false sense of security in a steady income stream from my job caused me to comfortably live paycheck to paycheck. Sure, I had a great time and lots of great memories, but no money! Because I had a steady paycheck coming in, I figured it was okay to spend all my money this week, knowing that I'd get paid again next week. No big deal. Plus, I have good credit now, so I'm in a good position. Right? Heck no! Looking back on my thinking now, I realize I was deceived, delusional, and delightfully ignorant. Better yet, let's call it what it really was – dumb: Don't Understand Money Boy.

I continued this pattern of spending and not saving during my five years and six months of active-duty service in the Navy right on into my civilian life when I was discharged. After I left the military, I relocated to Houston, TX and I purchased my first property which was a fourplex (a home with four apartments under one roof). One might ask how I was able to purchase a fourplex with no money saved. Great question. As a military veteran, we are able to purchase property with zero down payment. So, while I still had an income from the Navy, I purchased the home in Houston before I fully separated from the military. I lived in one of the units and the other 3 were rented out. I was good financially, so I thought.

Now keep in mind, so far, I only have five years of real adulthood experience where I was earning my own money and fully in control of it. But I had developed some bad spending habits. I had become addicted to maintaining a perfect credit score and I protected it at all costs. So here I am, 23 years old and I own my first investment property. I'm on my way to some serious wealth, right? Nope. Unfortunately, I still had not learned the importance of savings. Instead of putting money aside for savings, all the money that came in as profit from the rental units was used for my personal consumption. As a matter of fact, I spent the money even faster because it felt like free money that I didn't earn.

If you've ever owned property, you know that the property will eventually require maintenance and upkeep. Because I did not put aside money for maintenance and upkeep, I applied for credit cards from Home Depot and Best Buy to cover the cost of the items in need of repair. No surprise here, I was approved without a glitch because I had good credit. I replaced appliances as needed and made other small repairs using credit cards. I was able to maintain this for about two years before my financial foundation started crumbling beneath my feet and I felt the walls closing in on me. At this point, I was 26 years old and still had not learned how to prioritize saving money.

Then the unexpected happened. I had gotten behind on some credit card payments, I was losing my property to foreclosure while also being behind on the homeowner's association dues by several thousand dollars. Watching my financial life sink reminded me of what I learned from the movie the Titanic. The Titanic ship was supposedly unsinkable, but unfortunately while sailing it struck an iceberg that caused catastrophic damage to the ship and the ship ultimately sank. I thought my financial life was unsinkable, and I was confident that I was doing everything right. But unfortunately, I was wrong, and my financial ship was sinking and sinking fast. I had crashed into an iceberg of debt that took me out. My financial world as I knew it was over, and I was frantically fighting to stay afloat financially. I had to make some life altering decisions.

I had built my world around credit...not money. I viewed credit as my cash, but in actuality, credit was not cash at all. Instead, credit caused me to sink deeper and deeper into debt because I could not pay off the balances in full in order to avoid the compound interest for use of the credit cards. I had nowhere to turn. Bill collectors were calling me daily. I was going through foreclosure, which was stressful in and of itself. I had a 6-month-old son I had to take care of and as if that wasn't enough hardship for one person to bear, my father died in the midst of my financial calamity. With the weight of this stress and loss on my shoulders, I did something even more stupid than getting into debt in the first place. I borrowed $6000 from my aunt to try to prevent my property from going into foreclosure and to salvage my beloved credit score, all to no avail. ***(Side note: Never borrow money or make large financial decisions when you are afraid or stressed out. They usually end up bad.)*** So not only did I lose the house, but I added another $6000 to my debt load. Even though I didn't have to pay the mortgage because the house was foreclosed on, I still had to repay my aunt the $6000. It wasn't her fault I lost the property. I still owed her the money I had borrowed and promised to pay back. Even though my credibility was shot on my credit report, I did not want my credibility to be shot with my aunt who trusted me enough to loan me the money to get me out of a tight situation. So, I paid her back as part of my newfound appreciation for financial integrity.

This was a scary time in my life. I was mentally and physically overwhelmed by the financial pressure I was experiencing. The financial stress was so bad that it contributed to me having frequent debilitating headaches and ultimately a brain aneurysm. An aneurysm occurs when you have a blood vessel burst in your brain. When a medical condition such as this occurs, immediate death is the outcome about 90 percent of the time. The financial stress I was under had taken a serious toll on me and literally almost cost my life. I had to undergo brain surgery to repair the damage caused by the aneurysm and I spent about a month in the hospital recovering from surgery. Needless to say, this experience gave me a newfound appreciation and motivation for saving money. Perhaps if I had prioritized saving money sooner, I wouldn't have gotten behind on my financial obligations and this highly stressful situation wouldn't have happened. Or maybe if I had known how to handle and manage my money, I wouldn't have gotten myself into such a financial mess.

As you can see, my lack of intentionality in saving money while I had several opportunities to do so had catastrophic effects on my life. You may be wondering why I took the time to share my story with you. The answer is because I want you to know that I understand from a lived experience how harmful debt and lack of savings can be. I was never taught how to save growing up, so I was under-educated. And perhaps you've been under-educated, too. My hope is that reading my story will cause you to change the trajectory of your story moving forward. Your story may not be as dramatic as mine, but my guess is that there has been moments in your life when you've chosen not to save for whatever reason. Imagine how different your life could've been had you prioritized saving earlier on. While you can't necessarily redeem the time, you can start saving now as the first step in building wealth and living a life you're proud of.

So how do I start saving money?

During the many financial coaching sessions I've done over the years I've noticed a recurring theme. Most of my clients share similar stories wherein they were told that they needed to save money, but they were never told why they needed to save or shown how to save money in practical ways. Because they were never taught that saving is the foundation for building wealth, they never implemented a savings plan. And just as I've said to clients before, I'm saying this to you now: Saving money must become a top priority in your life. It is an EMERGENCY!

I often use the example of an emergency situation arising that requires you to obtain a large sum of money in a short amount of time. Imagine you have a loved one who has been diagnosed with an illness that will lead to certain death within six months if he or she don't get a cure. The cure is available, but it costs $10,000. You cannot borrow the money from family, friends or the hospital. You have to personally save $10,000 within 6 months to save your loved one's life. Would you do it? Admittedly, that's a lot of pressure for someone to endure and to some it may seem unrealistic. However, one hundred percent of the time, the answer is an emphatic YES when I'm face to face with my clients and I present them with this scenario. As a client reading this book now, what's your response to the question? Think of someone you love more than life itself and the only thing that would keep him or her alive is you coming up with $10,000.00. With those stipulations, do you think you could do it?

I then follow that scenario-based question up with another one-word question: HOW? Once they mentally commit to saving the amount of money necessary to save a loved one's life, all kinds of ideas and strategies emerge. I go on to point out to the people I'm speaking to that their income hasn't changed. The only thing that changed was their *motivation*. With the right motivation, they realized a lot of the money they spent was on non-essential items. With a willingness to make some sacrifices, they could achieve the goal of saving $10,000 and more importantly saving their loved one's life. As a coach, I simply break the goal down into bite-sized pieces. Example: $10,000 divided by 6 months is $1666.66 a month or $416.66 a week or $59.52 per day. The point of this exercise is to get them to see they have the ability to save, but ability without the right motivation is only half the battle. Their mind needed a compelling reason to make saving a priority. And the same is true for you. Once you embrace the ability to save and you have your "why" established as a reason to save, the next step is rid yourself of all the reasons you've accumulated over the years that justify you not saving. Once you get in the mindset of saving, then you start the habit of saving. When you hear the word habit, you probably think of doing something on a regular basis, which is correct.

To help you get in the habit of saving, I created an acronym for H.A.B.I.T.

HOURLY PAY – The H stands for HOURLY pay. I advise you to set aside one hour a day of your pay/salary and add it to your savings or emergency fund. Example: if you make $10 an hour and you work 40 hours a week, you should be saving $50 a week. If you work 8 hours a day, set aside one hour a day for your savings and learn to live off 7 hours of pay. Make whatever sacrifices you need to make because saving money has to become a priority.

ANNUAL GOAL – The A stands for setting ANNUAL financial goals. Based on you saving $50 a week, you should realistically be able to save $2600 a year. Will this make you rich? Not likely, but the point is to start the HABIT of saving. Your savings over time will grow into money that you can invest. The amount you choose to save each year does not have to comply with the numbers I used in the example. You can customize the dollar amount that applies to your life specifically. I encourage you not to procrastinate when it comes to setting your annual savings goal. Do it now. In fact, if it would be helpful, take a moment now to figure out the amount you want to save while it's fresh on your mind. Go ahead. I will wait. That's how important I think an annual savings goal is to building your wealth.

Got your number in mind? Assuming you said yes, go ahead and write that number down as your annual savings goal in a highly visible place and use it as motivation to keep you on track.

BUDGET – The B stands for BUDGETING your money. Budgeting allows you to tell your money where to go instead of wondering where it went. Establish a time when you can sit down and write out all your expenses and income on paper. Then put each dollar on a strict assignment with orders to comply with the budget and not deviate from the assignment under any circumstances. Your money needs to obey orders from you like a soldier obeys orders in the military. Make sure your money does what you've told it to do! The problem a lot of people have with managing their money is that they don't tell their money what to do. Consequently, their money tells *them* what *to do or,* more often than not, what *they* cannot *do.* I ask you the question: Who would you rather have in charge, you or your money?

INVEST – The I stands for INVEST your money. Accumulating money in your savings account is a good place to start. Eventually, however, you'll want to make sure your money starts replicating itself so you have money to invest. Remember, I talked about this earlier using compound interest. Let this concept marinate in your mind when it comes to your ability to invest and reap a return. Once you focus on growing your savings with the intent to invest it to grow your wealth, opportunities will seemingly begin to appear out of nowhere. The truth of the matter is opportunities to invest have always been there, but you were not focused on them. It's kind of like the phenomenon that happens when you purchase a new car. After you purchase the car, you start seeing the same type of car everywhere. Do you know why that happened? Because you were now focused on them. The cars didn't magically appear. They had always been there. You just weren't paying attention to them. But now that it's in your conscious mind, you will see them more often. It's the same with investment opportunities. When you purpose your mind to save in order to invest, you will start seeing investment opportunities everywhere.

TIME – The T stands for TIME. Time is one of those resources we don't fully appreciate until we don't have anymore. One of the benefits of prioritizing saving money is it puts you in position to free up your time. Having a substantial savings and your money invested earning more money allows you to do more than simply work all the time just to survive. Having more control over your time means you get to create more memories with the ones you love.

Plus, the sooner you start saving, the more time your money has to compound and grow. If two people were to start investing the same amount of money into the same type of investment account with the same rate of return of 10%, here's what would happen. Person A is 20 years old and invests $500 a month. Person B is 50 years old and invests $500 a month. After 30 years they both would have $995,688.94. Person A would be 50 years old and person B would be 80 years old. If person A continues for another 30 years with the same investment, simply because the 20-year-old started earlier, they would have $18,361,139.19 saved because of the extra time compound interest had to accumulate.

Lastly, there will come a "time" when you can no longer earn the way you do now and if you are unprepared financially, you will be left with only a few options. You will either be forced to live off what you invested in your younger years or be dependent on the government for assistance. Worst case, you become dependent on your children. I know most people don't anticipate this day or prepare for it, but trust me, it's coming. Be wise and prepare for it now. It's going to rain people. Have your financial umbrella ready.

Now that we've talked about the habit of saving money, let's talk about different ways you can use your savings to help with major purchases without needing to break the bank.

MAJOR PURCHASES: Helpful insights to know prior to buying big ticket items.

In an effort to offer some guidance to you that I didn't have in my younger years, this next section will focus on ways to navigate your way through making major purchases and to avoid pitfalls that await unsuspecting individuals. Let's start with buying a vehicle.

Buying A Car

When it comes to buying a vehicle, it will be helpful to answer the questions below before you ever set foot on a dealership lot. Here are a few.

- *What type of vehicle do you want (car, truck, SUV)?*
- *What's the purpose of the vehicle?*
- *Is fuel efficiency a concern?*
- *Do you want electric, hybrid or traditional gas engine?*
- *How much vehicle can you afford?*
- *Are you paying cash or financing?*
- *Are you committed to a particular brand of vehicle?*
- *How's the maintenance on the vehicle you're interested in?*
- *Is this particular vehicle a need or a want?*

After you've answered those questions, then you can proceed. With technology advancements, you can minimize time by shopping for a vehicle online first before going to the dealer to be haggled to death. I would recommend searching for the type of vehicle you are committed to buying online first. Check out reviews. Check out YouTube videos about the vehicle and learn from real owners about their experiences with the vehicle that are closer to reality than what the manufacturer or salesman will tell you. You can even search for and compare vehicles online now, which saves even more time. Most dealers have an active website where they keep an inventory of their vehicles online. Armed with information about what that particular vehicle is selling for makes you a more informed buyer and it helps to minimize the possibility of you paying too much for a vehicle. Of note, dealers usually have their lowest prices advertised online. Because they are trying to move their inventory, they offer the same vehicle at a reduced price online versus what you see on the sticker in the lot. Checking online first saves you money.

After you've answered the questions, did your research online and identified several vehicles to choose from, then it's time to prepare financially. If you're buying the vehicle with cash, that's awesome. Congratulations. You're winning with money. Always remember CASH IS KING! Also remember the salesman is there to sell vehicles. Period. You are there to buy it. Remove all emotions from the transaction. Never allow the salesman to sense you really want the vehicle. Once they detect that you're emotionally attached to a specific vehicle, you've pretty much surrendered many of your negotiating powers.

Stick to the facts and say something like this 'I want this vehicle, and this is how much I'm willing to pay you for it. I'm paying with cash, and I don't need to wait for approval. Do you want to make this sale, or should I talk to another sales person?' This spiel comes off hard and insensitive, but you're not at the dealership to make friends. You're there to purchase a vehicle. I'm not saying you should be a jerk. By all means, be cordial and respectful, but stay focused on the goal. The salesperson came to work to sell a vehicle to a stranger who showed up to their lot. They don't know you. And although you are having an interaction with a person, the transaction isn't personal at all. Keep it professional and stay about the business.

Just a word of caution; there will be times when your cash offer will be rejected. That's ok. Remember it's not personal. If your offer is rejected, you then have two choices. Either renegotiate or walk away with your cash and find another vehicle at a different dealership. Some vehicles are priced right and that's just what it is. If you want it, buy it. You're not necessarily taking a loss if you pay what they are asking for the vehicle – especially if you've done your research prior to getting to the dealer. You should have a good feeling about the pricing.

I remember my last vehicle I purchased was a Lexus LS 460. I had been looking for one online for over 6 months. It wasn't a vehicle I needed, but it was a vehicle that I wanted. Because it was a desire and not a need, I didn't feel rushed to make the purchase. Also, I was buying it with cash. One day while looking online, I saw the vehicle I wanted. It was beautiful and in nearly brand-new condition. The paint was flawless with no nicks or scratches. The seats looked as if they'd never been sat on. It was perfect in every way. It had just hit the market, so I instantly went to check it out in person. It even looked better in person than it did in the pictures. I drove it to my mechanic to check it out before proceeding. Everything checked out. Time to negotiate.

This car was priced three thousand dollars lower than any others that I had seen that were comparable to it. I had already seen the online price before going to the dealership. When I got there, of course the sticker price was $1500 more than what I saw online. After informing them that I was aware of the online price and I was paying in cash, I was like, I'm ready to make a deal. The manager politely informed me that my cash was somewhat irrelevant because they priced it online at absolute rock bottom pricing just to sell it quickly. I then had a decision to make. Was I going to allow my pride and ego to influence me to leave because the dealer wasn't going to give me a better deal and they had rejected my offer, or was I going to accept the fact that this car was in excellent condition, had no mechanical issues, and was already priced $3000 lower than any others that I'd seen? You know what I did? What any other man with the ability to check his pride and ego at the door would have done. I went to my bank and got the cash to buy it. It was a win-win situation for all parties. I didn't feel like I was taken advantage of. I got what I wanted, and they made a sale.

Being informed and prepared when you are making such large purchases is what will make this process smoother and prevent you from being stuck with buyers' remorse (that feeling you get after you buy something you don't need, or you feel like you overpaid for and now you regret buying it).

If you're purchasing a vehicle and you're going to use financing (borrowing money), try to obtain financing approval prior to going to the dealer. Either from a bank or your credit union if you have one. It will make you a much stronger buyer and it will set some parameters on what you can and are willing to spend. It can be helpful to go to the dealership with a predetermined amount you're willing to spend on a vehicle. Waiting until you get to the dealership and relying on the dealer to provide financing puts you at a disadvantage, as the likelihood of you becoming emotionally attached to a vehicle you see on the lot may hinder your ability to make a financially wise decision. Once your excitement for a particular vehicle is apparent, you're done, as the salesperson will likely try to upsell you to the vehicle you like or another comparable car that you can "afford" the payments on. They ask questions like "How much do you want to pay a month?" as if they are concerned about your budget. They are not even remotely concerned about your financial well-being. They are trying to see what car they can fit you in based on the monthly payment. And since they are doing the financing, they can easily manipulate the numbers to "force" the vehicle you want into your budget. Don't fall for this tactic. They're not necessarily trying to harm you; they're just trying to make a sale. Playing on your emotions can cause you to make a quick decision to buy the vehicle because of how you feel about the vehicle, and perhaps, what the vehicle says about your status. Instead of logic and reason having a seat at the decision-making table, they are sent to wait outside while you and the salesperson are waiting on your financing approval to come back.

Buying from an individual vs dealer.

If you're planning on purchasing a used vehicle from an individual, be extra cautious. These can be great, or they can be a nightmare. I'm not opposed to buying from individuals if you have some experience purchasing cars. If it's your first time, I'd say get one from a reputable dealer. Ignorance is expensive. Your lack of knowledge can cost you money and unwanted headaches. Here are a few things to check for if you do decide to purchase from an individual.

- Make sure they have the title (document showing who legally owns a vehicle) to the vehicle in their name and possession.
- Make sure the name on the title matches the name on the driver's license.
- Take the vehicle to a local trusted mechanic shop and ask them to do a quick examination of the vehicle to ensure there aren't any hidden issues with the vehicle that can't be seen from the outside.
- Drive the vehicle with the radio off. This will help you hear any strange noises while driving.
- Use the power of cash to negotiate a good deal but try to be fair and reasonable. You don't want to use cash as a bashing tool to beat people down with.

I personally would recommend buying a used vehicle over a new one. Wealthy people purchase slightly used vehicles with moderately low (50k-100k) miles on them. That's one way they maintain their wealth. They don't invest large sums of money in things that don't maintain their value. Unless you're rich and can afford to throw away thousands of dollars just so you can be the first person to drive it and for the "new car smell" it has, it may be wiser to purchase a pre-owned vehicle. A new car typically loses over 60% of its value within the first 3 to 5 years. For a visual aid, imagine every Monday morning on the way to work, pulling out of your garage, rolling down the windows and throwing two $100 bills out for the next three years.

Buying a brand-new car is a terrible investment. Why? Depreciation. What is that? Depreciation is the opposite of Appreciation. Appreciation is when something goes up in value over time (homes, stocks, precious metals, etc.). Depreciation then is when something goes down in value over time (vehicles, clothing, electronics, etc.) So, vehicle depreciation is the difference between what you paid when you bought the vehicle and what you are able to sell it for. As you drive the vehicle and put more mileage and wear and tear on it, the more it goes down in value.

Example: Say you bought a vehicle for $20,000.00 today. Three years later, you decide to sell it. At a 40% value loss ($8000.00), the most you could get for your vehicle would be about $12,000.00. Now here's the trap that gets a lot of people locked up in the prison of vehicle poverty for years. Let's use the same vehicle you bought today for $20,000. Three years later you may "need" or desire a new car, but you've only paid down the principal balance by only $5000. So, in essence, you still have a balance of $15,000 for the vehicle that's only worth $12,000.00. You see the problem here? All of a sudden, you now have a negative balance of $3000.00 that you still owe the lender for the vehicle. In the auto world, that's called being "upside down" on your car.

Most people aren't aware of this dangerous pitfall until it happens to them. Out of pure ignorance, they panic. And we all know it's rare for people to make good quality decisions when they are in panic mode. Remember me borrowing $6000 from my aunt to save my property from foreclosure earlier? I panicked. So what ends up happening when a person tries to switch out their old vehicle for a newer one? They go back to the dealer to purchase a new vehicle for $25,000, but they still owe $3000, so now the new vehicle they financed has a total cost of $28,000.00. Why? Because they had to add the old balance of $3000 to the new balance of $25,000. Unfortunately, the same thing will happen to this vehicle as well in three years. It too will lose value quickly. You see how this cycle gets people further in debt when financing vehicles. By now that "new car smell" is not so appealing. It actually stinks! But you're stuck with the payments and the financial aftermath of a vehicle that no longer appeals to you or your "fans". There are thousands of people stuck in this vicious cycle of being upside down on auto loans. Sadly, for many, this has become normal – And it's because they don't know any better and haven't been exposed to anything different. They are UNDER EDUCATED.

Buying Your First Home

As critical as this step is to life, wealth and stability, there wasn't one class I took in high school or college that taught me anything about buying a home or the benefits of owning real estate. Buying a home is a significant part of adulting and it was never mentioned by anyone in my educational journey. It's almost like the things that actually create wealth are overlooked in our educational system.

As an active real estate broker, it has become the sole mission of my company Investment Scouts Realty, to educate and help individuals get into real estate ownership. I'm passionate about helping people build wealth through owning real estate. After all, long before the stock market, tech companies, entertainers and viral social media videos were making people wealthy, real estate was one of the primary methods of building and transferring wealth. I'm convinced real estate ownership has to be credited for creating the most millionaires in history. And what makes owning real estate even better is the barrier to entry is very low. You don't need an advanced degree, or to come from a royal family lineage. You don't need to have a large amount of money either. All you need is a job/source of income, good credit history, and some funds for a down payment. That's really all you need to get into the game. Are you excited yet? Let's get into it a little deeper.

Why should I buy a home?

Well, the first answer is quite obvious. You need somewhere to live. But beyond that, there are many advantages and benefits of owning a home. One is freedom and peace of mind. When you own a home, you don't have to worry about having a landlord who may decide to sell the home and force you to relocate, or have annual increases of your rent. For my creatives, you get to add your own touch to the décor to make your house feel like a home.

Another reason to purchase a home is because it's an easy way to build equity. Equity is a commonly used term in real estate that simply means the difference in what you owe on your home and what the home's current worth or appraised property value is. Equity is money earned from a home's appreciation (increasing in value) over time. Example, if you have a $200,000 home and the balance you owe is $150,000 then you have $50,000 in equity. Depending on where you live, the value may increase faster than other homes. That's why in real estate, you hear these three words often: LOCATION, LOCATION, LOCATION. Where the home is located has a major impact on its current value and potential future value.

There are many tax advantages to owning a home. I'm not a Certified Public Accountant (CPA), so I won't risk overstepping my boundaries here, as each state may have different laws. However, there are some benefits I can speak to, such as interest. You get to write off interest paid to a mortgage, property taxes or origination points and you can deduct your home office as a business expense. All of these deductions offset the taxes you pay on your taxable earned income for the year. You don't get any of these benefits as a renter.

Another reason to buy a home is you can kickstart your rental portfolio. You can get started building wealth slowly through home ownership. That's what I did. I told you about my first property which was a fourplex. My second property was a duplex (2-unit home). I moved into one side and rented the other side out. The rent from the other side covered 90% of my mortgage expenses. It was like I was living for free. I stayed in that house for 5 years before buying my first free standing home as my primary residence. I slowly built my real estate portfolio over time. Now, I currently have six homes and collect rent from all but the one I live in. I only have a mortgage on two of my six homes and there's significantly more equity in them than the balance owed on them. I have tenants helping me build my wealth because I started buying real estate early. I have intentions of buying more rental properties when the right deal becomes available.

Things to consider when buying a home.

When considering a home to purchase, start by determining the area you would like to live in. How much can you afford? Are school districts important to you? How many bedrooms do you need? Do you want a single-story home or two-story home? How close do you want to be to your place of employment? Do you want to live close to a lot of people in the city or out in the suburbs? Is the house you are considering in an area that will increase in value? How's the crime in the area? Do you want a house that may need a little work, or would you prefer a brand-new home that has never been lived in?

As you are refining your search and getting closer to finding the house that's right for you, start to drive the neighborhood at night to see how it looks. Would you feel safe coming to your home at night? The things you see as you drive into the area are the same things others will see when it's time to sell your home. So be mindful of the area.

I encourage you NOT to purchase the largest, nicest home in the neighborhood. The reason I encourage you not to buy the largest house in the neighborhood is because if you have the largest home in the area, the home has little room to increase in value. It will increase, but slower than others.

One of the reasons for this is the people who would be your potential buyers aren't looking to buy in that price range in that neighborhood. Let me explain it like this. Let's say you live in a neighborhood where the homes range from $200,000 to $300,000. You buy a home at $350,000 in the neighborhood because it's significantly larger than the other homes in the area and it has a bigger yard, pool, etc. That's nice, but potential buyers looking in that neighborhood aren't looking to spend $350,000. They are looking to spend $250,000. Therefore, your home will be out of the price range for the majority of the people looking to purchase in that area. I advise you to try and purchase on the low end of the neighborhood value instead of the high end. By doing this, you increase your equity potential. There's more room to go up in equity for a rising community than buying at the top.

So, is renting a home bad?

Not at all. Renting a home is not a bad thing. There's a time and place for renting, and there's nothing inherently wrong with renting. Renting an apartment or home after you graduate from high school or college is perfectly fine, as you likely won't have enough money to purchase a home during the early stages of adulthood. However, I caution you against renting as a way of life long-term. Renting should be a transitional living situation. For example, if you are just moving to a new city or you're only planning to be in the new city for a short amount of time, renting is perfectly acceptable.

Even though you may be renting for a season, I encourage you to work diligently to get your finances in order so you can position yourself to become a homeowner. Remember, there are multiple benefits that come from home ownership. You don't want to miss out on those benefits. Check out this next scenario.

Consider this tale of two neighbors who live next door to each other in similar homes. One is a renter and the other is a homeowner. Both homes are valued at $200,000.00. Both neighbors pay the same amount of money each month ($1000.00) to live in their homes. Both have access to the same community amenities. Their children attend the same great schools. After 10 years, the renter has paid in cash money $120,000.00 in rent. When he chooses to leave the house and not renew his rental contract, he may get his security deposit back, if he is lucky. The homeowner has paid $120,000.00 in cash as well. However, he has been paying down the principal balance (original amount borrowed) of the home while also building equity. Ten years later, the homeowner's home is now worth $280,000.00. When he decides to sell his home, he will walk away with between $80,000.00 to $100,000.00 cash after paying commissions, title fees, etc. Do you see the money being given away or missed out on as a renter? Do you see why those who are homeowners can build wealth faster? The only difference between these two neighbors was that one owned his home and the other rented the home. Again, there's nothing wrong with renting, but you miss out on the financial gains and benefits of owning a home. We have been UNDER EDUCATED!

When should I consider buying a home?

The answer to this question is based on your finances. Let's say you are financially ready at the age of 20. Great. If you bought a home and paid it off on schedule with a 30-year mortgage, you would have it paid off by the time you were 50 years old. Not bad. Now imagine you purchased a home at the age of 20 and paid it off in 15 years which is what I usually recommend, then you will have a paid off home at the young age of 35. By paying off your first home, you have put yourself in a position to build some serious wealth with 30-40 years with no mortgage payment. If you'd like to learn more about how to pay your mortgage off faster and save tons of money on interest payments, I invite you to read my book *Unlock Your Mind, Unlock your Money*.

Should my first home be my dream home?

No. Stop dreaming and get back to reality. Just kidding. My first home was a home that allowed me to live in it for free. My second home did the same thing. I didn't purchase my first single family home until 10 years after I purchased my multi-family homes. But I know most people are not going to buy a multi-family property to live in like I did. I encourage you to consider starting with a small "starter" home that is functional and meets your needs. When it comes to your first home, you don't have to buy this spectacular home that gives you goosebumps every time you pull up to the house. Remember, this is a starter home and the main point is functionality and putting yourself in a better financial situation in the future so you can invest in other wealth building opportunities. I'm not saying you have to buy a home in a bad area that you're afraid to live in or that is zoned to an underperforming school district and you're concerned about your children's education. I'm simply encouraging you to think about the big picture concerning your finances, so you can position yourself to build wealth over the long term.

If you are single or a married couple with no children, I would recommend buying a small home to start off with. Live in it until you've outgrown it, need to relocate, or you're positioned to afford something nicer because your income has increased. Unfortunately, the problem a lot of people have is their appetite for a home is too large for their income. They end up "house rich and cash poor," meaning they bought more home than they could realistically and comfortably afford. Don't be like those people.

Purchasing a home is not a race and it's not about flexing. It's about putting yourself in a position to build wealth over time. You're not marrying the house. You're not stuck with it "til death do you part." There will always be a home for sale that you could upgrade to later. I promise. In the meantime, begin with a starter home and then upgrade when you're financially ready. As part of the lifestyle upgrade, you could transition your first home to become rental property where tenants are now paying the mortgage. Now you have two homes building equity instead of one. If, however, you don't want to be a landlord, you could sell the first home and use the equity from it to put a larger down payment on the next home. Either way, you're winning.

What are the minimum requirements to buy a home?

Great question. As mentioned earlier, I'm an active real estate broker and I've been selling homes for over 17 years as of this writing. I have some experience in this. So, for starters, you will need to be able to show proof of a steady source of income. This could be from a job, pension, disability letter, or your small business income. The lender will need to be able to verify your income. They will also look at your credit score. There are a lot of lenders who offer different financing terms with varying credit scores. The lowest I've seen was a minimum score of 580. Now keep in mind what we talked about earlier. The lower your credit score, the more likely the lender is to consider you a high risk and penalize you. They will loan you the money, but you will pay a higher interest rate than someone with a 750-credit score. The difference in what lenders offer in terms of interest rates can vary from 1% to 3% which, on a mortgage, can result in a drastic difference in what you will pay monthly for the same exact home. We're talking as much as $300 or more a month. Do the math over 30 years and see how much a low credit score costs you. This is why staying on top of your finances is critical, as it impacts many areas of life in not so obvious ways.

You will also need money for a down payment, which is the amount of money you put down towards the principal balance of the home. This reinforces my point about having some money saved. When it comes to major purchases, having money saved will be very helpful and makes the process much better.

When purchasing a home, you will likely need to secure a loan. If you're a military veteran, you could secure a VA loan, which allows you to purchase a home with zero down payment. However, you still have to meet all the other qualifications as far as income, credit score, employment, etc. You could also secure a Fair Housing Administration (FHA) loan. This loan type was created to help people become homeowners by reducing the down-payment amount to 3.5% of the purchase price. For example, if you're trying to purchase a home for $200.000.00, your down payment amount would be $7000.00. This type of loan, along with the VA loan, is a federally backed or guaranteed loan. In essence, the government is saying to the lender (usually a large bank) that if this person gets behind on his or her payments and loses the home to foreclosure, it (the federal government) will be responsible for any portion of the balance that isn't collected as a result of selling the home at a foreclosure auction.

Another common loan type is the "conventional" loan. Obtaining a conventional involves simply going directly to a bank and borrowing the money you need for your purchase. This type of loan is not guaranteed by the government; thus, it's used more frequently used with people who have excellent credit, excellent income, and stable employment. Because the borrower is viewed more favorably, the lender views them as less risky and can offer more competitive interest rates.

Next order of business is getting pre-qualified with a lender for a loan. This pre-qualification is the process where a lender gathers your financial information, verifies your employment, checks your credit, and verifies your income sources. This is the beginning of the process of determining if you are going to be able to obtain a loan from a mortgage bank. After you've met with a lender to get pre-qualified, you're ready to start looking at homes. Your lender will tell you how much home you can afford based on your income, credit, etc.

Contact a good realtor who is knowledgeable of the market in the area and let him/her know what you're looking for. Once you identify a home you'd like to purchase, have your realtor to submit a written contract to purchase the home, then the next phase of the process begins. You will need some upfront cash, in addition to the money you have in reserves for the down payment we mentioned earlier. Here are the things you will have to pay for out of pocket up front.

Earnest Money. This is a term used in real estate that means you put a certain amount of money down as a way to express your interest in purchasing the home. The earnest money tells the seller that you're serious about purchasing the home. It's like a security deposit. The earnest money amount typically ranges from $500 to $1000 and is typically collected by the title company, a third-party entity that facilitates the transfer of ownership from the seller to the buyer. The earnest money is typically placed in an escrow account. Some selling agents require a percentage of the overall sales price of the home you are purchasing – usually, between 1% and 2%. For easy math, let's use the same purchase price from earlier of $200,000.00. A 1% earnest money deposit would be $2000.00, and a 2% earnest money deposit would be $4000.00.

Option money: Option money is usually a small amount of money you put down in exchange for the seller giving you time to do your due diligence concerning the property without obligating you to a binding contract. Essentially, the option money says to the seller that you're serious about purchasing the home; however, because you don't know much about it, you want the "option" to terminate this contract if you discover something wrong with it during a specified time period (usually 7-10 days after signing the contract) and we can't reach an agreement to have it fixed. Option money gives you the option to change your mind about purchasing the home. Both the earnest money and option money will be given back to you as a credit once you close on (purchase) the property. If you terminate the contract within the pre-established option period, you forfeit your option money, and the seller retains it in exchange for taking the home off the market from other potential buyers while you had it under contract. However, you get your earnest money back if the contract is terminated within the time frame specified in the contract. During the "option period," you would have an independent inspector come to the home and conduct a thorough inspection.

Home Inspections: Speaking of inspections, that's another cost you will have to pay upfront. I highly recommend having a licensed inspector come out and conduct a home inspection to all of my buyers. They check for things like electrical issues, plumbing issues, foundation issues, heating and cooling, roof conditions, and more. Inspections are there to help give you peace of mind about purchasing the home. Inspection fees can range anywhere from $300 to $700 depending on the area and size of the home. After completing the inspection, the inspector will meet with you and share information about any defects they discovered. And trust me, they will find some. Don't be too alarmed by this. No home is perfect. The inspection report you receive can be used to ask the seller to make some necessary repairs or adjust the sales price in light of the repairs needed. Of course, there is no guarantee that the seller *will* make any of the requested repairs or adjust their asking price. However, having the report in hand usually serves as incentive because it provides hard evidence from a neutral party regarding the condition of the home.

Appraisal Fee: The appraisal fee is paid to an independent appraiser who goes to the home, verifies that it exists and determines the value of the home based on similar homes in the area that have sold. Generally speaking, appraisal fees are paid in advance by the buyer, although there are some lenders who will pay for them and roll them into the closing costs. Appraisal fees tend to vary, but using our $200,000.00 figure from above, you can assume the fee will be approximately $500.00. Appraisers are contracted by the lender and their job is to assure the lender that the money they are about to loan for the property is actually a good loan and the property is worth the amount agreed upon in the contract. There are times when the appraisal value will come back higher than the amount agreed upon in the contract. This means you instantly have equity in the home before you even purchase it. Isn't that wonderful? There are also times when the appraisal value will come back lower than the agreed upon purchase price in the contract. If this happens, the seller is faced with a tough choice. Either refund the earnest money and terminate the contract or lower the price to the appraised amount. This is rare, but it does happen. It just happened to me recently on a home I was selling.

That sums up all the upfront costs associated with buying a home. I can't tell you the number of people I've helped buy a home over the years who were hesitant to purchase or even begin the purchase process because they were UNDER-EDUCATED about the home buying process. They simply didn't know how easy it could be to buy a home. While there are multiple components to buying a home, the home buying process from start to finish can be completed within 30-45 days on average.

Should you use a realtor?

Yes! When buying, selling or leasing a home, I strongly encourage you to use a licensed realtor to help you navigate the process. Buying and selling real estate is not for the novice. There are a lot of details that must be adhered to and there is a lot of money involved. As a buyer, it doesn't cost you anything to have a realtor representing you in the transaction. Your realtor will be compensated by the seller or owner of the property. Their fees are already factored into the sales price. And yes, even if you are buying a brand-new home from a builder, you still should have a realtor on your team to ensure you are getting the best deal and are not being taken advantage of.

When you are selling a home, you will pay the realtor a fee to list (sell) your home. The listing fee includes compensation for the selling agent to market the home to potential qualified buyers, review and negotiate contracts, advise the seller, etc. As mentioned earlier, the buyer's agent will be compensated from this fee as well. This fee is usually warranted because the realtor will work to get you the most money for your home. One thing is for sure, whether you are buying or selling a home, having a knowledgeable professional realtor on your team is an investment you can't afford to miss out on.

BONUS TIP: Things you should not do when in the process of buying a home.

Once you've decided to purchase a home and have begun the home buying process, absolutely do not do any of the following:

- Do not apply for any new credit/debt. Doing so will impact your debt-to-income ratio. Remember, we talked about this earlier.
- Don't buy a new vehicle. This too will impact your debt-to-income ratio.
- Do not deposit large sums of cash in your account that you don't want the lender to ask questions about or whose source you don't want to document and explain. Large deposits into a buyer's account prior to the purchase of a home are a red flag to the lender that looks like potential money laundering.
- Do not change jobs or careers. When the lender gives you a pre-approval, it's based on documents you've already provided. If you go and change jobs, this may impact the decision they previously made based on new changes to your employment and potentially income. An exception to this would be if you are a schoolteacher and you change to a school counselor, then that would be fine. It's still in the same line of work. But if you wanted to start selling your grandmother's famous sweet potato pies from a food truck, that's probably not a good idea. This will delay the process and create a lot of unnecessary frustration.

I hope these insights have been helpful to you thus far. I have plenty more to share. Keep reading. I promise it will be worth your time.

LIFE LESSON TWO

Career Choices – How Will You Earn Your Money?

Choosing the right career.

One of the essential questions we all have to ask in life is: What will we do to earn income? Whether you choose to live as a single person all of your life or decide to have a family, we still have to determine how we will take care of our basic financial needs and wants. In this section, I will attempt to discuss options for you to consider as you are on your journey to answer the question of how will you earn money.

Do you want to pursue a traditional career like a lawyer, doctor, teacher, nurse, mechanic, administrator, or are you looking for something different? Will the career you choose require higher education from a university or can you go straight into the workforce?

Choose a career that fits the lifestyle you desire.

How do you make an informed decision about such a significant part of life like choosing your career? I say choose your career as you consider the following. First, how will this career lend itself to the lifestyle you desire to live? If you create the lifestyle you want to live before choosing a career, your odds of being fulfilled by the career choice are significantly higher. Many people don't think about this aspect of choosing a career until after the fact. They simply choose based on the dollars. They are attracted by the salary and earning potential. But sometimes, your quality of life and the freedoms you desire have to outweigh the income.

For example, I was offered a job once working at a prominent law firm doing investigative work because of my police background and experience. The salary was really good, and it came with a full benefits package, plus annual bonuses. On the surface it sounded like a dream job, and for me, it was just that, a dream job. If I had taken that job, I would have worked 50-60 hours a week and would only have two weeks off annually for vacation. I would have had to wear a suit or dress business casual to work daily and contend with the god-awful traffic twice a day, five days a week. For me, that didn't fit the lifestyle I wanted to live.

By turning that job down, I avoided the potential of years of my life wasted on a job that I didn't want and that I was pursuing strictly based upon the money and benefits it offered. Accepting that job and having to modify my lifestyle to meet the work-related commitments it would have required would not have been good for me or the law firm I would have been working for.

One thing I've always known is that I don't want to ever feel stuck on a job that doesn't bring me fulfillment. I enjoy my freedom. I enjoy freedom to choose when I want to work. I enjoy being rewarded based off of my productivity. Thus, the lifestyle of an entrepreneur is more fitting for me personally or at least a job that has flexibility and some autonomy. This doesn't mean there was anything wrong with working the other job, but for me and how I want to live my life, it wasn't the best fit. I'm more comfortable with uncertainty because I know the earning potential is higher. The life of an entrepreneur has no income ceiling, and you can truly earn as much as your efforts produce. However, there's not a base or income foundation either. Thus, just as you can earn as much income as your efforts produce, you can earn as little as your efforts produce.

Now, please keep this in mind. I wasn't turning down the job without having savings and income already in place to sustain my lifestyle. I had passive income coming in and was earning sufficient money from my real estate sales to live comfortably. I wasn't just sitting at home watching television and eating cookies. When you're broke and unemployed, you don't have the luxury of a job "not fitting your lifestyle" because you're broke! Go to work. Any work. Until you can get on your feet and create some cushion between you and life's expenses, you can't afford to be picky. This clarification is just in case someone read this and interpreted the wrong thing. I don't want to mislead anyone into thinking I'm giving them permission to be lazy in the name of choosing a career that fits their lifestyle. Nope, not happening. Get to work!

College, Trade School or Military? What are the Pro's and Con's?

This section of the book may be most relevant for young adults and their parents. If you're between the age of 17-24 years old, or the parent of a teenager in high school, this particular chapter is very important. It can give you insights and a perspective on life choices not thoroughly discussed in school.

After graduating from high school, many students are at a pivotal point in life. They have some say-so regarding the direction they would like their lives to take and it's a time when they are able to make decisions that are not totally dictated by their parents. They can choose whether they want to go to college or go into the workforce. This can be an exciting time for students and parents alike. Both the student and the parents are excited about the same thing for once. Freedom! Most of the parents I know have been preparing their children for this moment in time since they started kindergarten. The high school graduation is the mile marker in life that indicates your exit is near and it's time to leave the house.

Thus, graduation is the first major life milestone for children and parents who are eagerly, yet cautiously, preparing to send their children off to learn and implement the things they were taught over the last 18 years. They've been armed with 12 years of formal education. Now what? Should they go to college, join the military, go to trade school, or go directly into the workforce? These young people are faced with choosing which direction they will travel, and they are standing at the intersection of life where the choice they make can and will impact the rest of their lives.

Today, many students are encouraged and expected to go straight to college after graduating high school for more education and the potential to secure a higher paying job in the marketplace. When choosing a college, consider the following before committing. Is a degree required for what I want to do? How much will this education cost? How am I going to pay for it? Where will I attend college? What are the projected career options after I complete the degree? Is this what I want or am I being led by some outside influence. Will the financial investment in a college degree payoff and increase my earning potential enough to make the investment of time and student loan debt worth it? Let's talk about it a little deeper.

Caution: Some may experience a bit of turbulence here; however, we should clear it fairly quickly. Just keep your seatbelts fastened for me. Don't abort the journey.

Also, just so we're on the same page, it is my belief that, at its core, the primary reason to obtain a college education is to increase earning potential. I mean, would people voluntarily exchange 4-6 more years of their life, along with several thousand dollars to study, read, and do exams purely for knowledge's sake? Very few would do this. I believe people go to college primarily to increase their earning potential. Is that the same assumption you have? That's the premise from which I will be discussing this topic.

Before we go any further, let me just state plainly – I am all for knowledge and higher education. I'm not anti-education by any means. I just want to ensure that those considering this path have a clear picture of what it will cost in totality before getting in and discovering this is not what they want. By then, the damage has already begun, the debt snowball is already rolling and it will be hard to get back on track. I want to raise your awareness and possibly prevent unnecessary financial stress. With that being said, let's talk about it.

The first thing we need to discuss is what do you want to do to earn money and whether it requires a college degree to do so. If you're pursuing a career as an attorney, engineer, architect or in the medical field, college is mandatory. Those are specialized fields that require a college education to be able to perform those functions as a competent professional. If you have a passion for a career in a specialized field, then choosing a college is a must. However, if your desire is in sales, or service type jobs, a college degree may not be a requirement.

The trap many fall into is the belief that the only path to financial success is by obtaining a college degree. That simply is not true. A college degree has many benefits and if that's something you desire for knowledge in a particular area in order to increase your income earning potential, great. But please understand the secret to building wealth is not tied to a university. I know plenty of broke people with college degrees from Associates to Doctorates. And I know plenty of wealthy people who have never stepped on a college campus.

How much will this advanced education cost?

Once you've determined that the career path you want to pursue in life requires advanced education and training, the next step is to identify where you want to obtain the knowledge and how much it will cost you to obtain it.

The cost of a college education continues to rise. Some research suggests college tuition has consistently increased faster than inflation. Basically, on average, college tuition increases by 5 -8 percent annually. Every year, the same education will cost more money to obtain. Oh, by the way, I'm not sure if you were aware or not, but COLLEGE UNIVERSITIES ARE BUSINESSES! They are for profit entities and institutions. The more prestigious the college or university is, the more it will cost to attend. It's almost like you're paying for the association, similar to paying for name brand products. You're paying for the name and the prestige associated with the school.

With that being said, determine the cost. One piece of advice I give clients with teenagers is to see what preliminary courses can be taken at a junior college or local community college. Obtaining an undergraduate degree requires some fundamental core courses that are transferrable. Taking this route can save you thousands of dollars by allowing you to complete some of the core course work at the community college and transferring to a university of choice to complete the remaining classes.

Parents be mindful of this cost saving step because the average high school graduate likely will not be thinking about the costs associated with an advanced education. As we've already discussed, the child at this point is so excited about their newfound freedom and tasting independence that they don't stop to think about the cost. They very likely don't even know to think about this. They are just ready to go.

What about a scholarship? If you are fortunate enough to get a scholarship, that's awesome. Take full advantage of it. Many colleges offer athletic scholarships to students who excel in sports as well as academic scholarships to students who excel academically. This is why maintaining good grades during high school is important. Those efforts to keep and maintain good grades can come in handy when seeking scholarships for college. Colleges seek to recruit students who they believe has the academic discipline to complete their program. So, apply for as many scholarships as you can. You may get lucky.

Most people will not be fortunate enough to get a scholarship. Thus, many will take out student loans to pay for college.

The student loan trap

What is a student loan? Its money loaned by the Federal government or other lending institutions to a student who wishes to attend college but does not have the resources to pay for the tuition out of pocket with their own money. The loan will usually pay for the tuition, books and on campus housing. The money is paid to the college directly on behalf of the student borrowing it. The college tuition for the semester is paid upfront by the lender before the student can begin taking classes. The lender will continue to loan money to the student as long as they are enrolled in school. This loan is then expected to be repaid upon graduation from college by the student. I believe there's a grace period given to allow the student who has just graduated time to find employment. There's also an extended period to delay repayment that can be requested by the student which is called deferment.

Deferment simply means to "delay or put off." Millions of college graduates take advantage of this option of deferment due to the amount of debt they accumulated over the four-year college period. Be mindful that while the loan payments are not due immediately, the interest charged is still accumulating. Which means the amount you owe is constantly rising even though you don't have to make payments right away.

Student loans has served as a resource to help many people obtain education at a college level that ultimately qualified them for jobs and opportunities, they would not have had without the college education. Many people have been able to elevate their families out of poverty because they were able to obtain a higher paying job that otherwise wouldn't have been available to them without a degree. Certainly, the student loans have helped a lot of people in very positive ways. But like any other debt, there's a dark side that lurks in the shadows.

Student loans are one of the leading causes of depression among many young adults. "*The burden of debt also contributes to acute mental health issues, including prolonged stress, anxiety, and feelings of shame. A 2021 mental health survey indicated 1 in 14 borrowers experienced suicidal ideation in response to the financial stress of student loans. This stress cannot be therapized away."* This quote was taken from **www.clasp.org** in a blog titled The Psychological Toll of Student Debt. Here are a few traps that come with student loans that both the students and parents should look out for and avoid when possible.

Trap #1: More than enough

The Financial Aid department or entity loaning students money for college will loan you more than you need for tuition. I believe they call it a ***refund***. Do you see how deceptive this word is? When we hear refund, it sounds like free money or money that's owed to us. But in this case, it's actually excess money unused from the financial aid payment after all the tuition costs, room and board, etc., are taken out. To the unknowing and unaware young 18-year-old student, it's an extra $5000 – $10000 in free money. I guess the lenders are being generous because they are concerned about your personal well-being, so they give you several thousand dollars more than you actually need for room and board, tuition and books. (Insert sarcastic laugh) If you're currently in college or planning to attend college, don't accept the "refund." That's not a REFUND...IT'S A LOAN! You will have to pay all that money back with interest. It's a TRAP!!!

Trap #2: You can't get rid of it.

One of the causes of the lenders extreme generosity is because they are legally protected. Student loans are the only loans that I'm aware of that are exempt from bankruptcy filing. Basically, you can't file for bankruptcy to dismiss your student loans. They are going to be a part of your life until you either pay them off or die. With this level of security, of course lenders will loan you money for college. They will be earning interest for many years to come.

Trap #3: Greed begets more greed.

This easy money of course contributed to the actual cost of tuition increasing as well. Remember, many of the schools are for profit institutions. They see thousands of students are getting easy money earmarked for them, so why would you think greed wouldn't make an appearance and claim more of this easy money. Schools raise the cost of tuition, textbooks, etc., and lenders are willing to loan the money. Every year the cycle starts over again. The costs are largely unregulated, and the benefits have been marketed so well, that people don't even stop to think about it until after they've already been consumed by debt.

The trap is now set.

It's a perfect storm brewing. Student was told "go to school, get good grades so you can get a good job." Because the student desires to earn more money, they enroll in college. Now keep in mind the student is broke, under educated and without a job, but based on the effective marketing of the idea that a college degree will practically guarantee a higher paying job, the student takes out thousands of dollars in student loans. The lenders don't see a problem with loaning this much money to an 18-year-old. After all, the loan is literally secured by the life of the recipient. Student gets approved for tuition and the school gets paid upfront. Whether this education actually produces what it promised is irrelevant. That's totally up to the student now. As far as the schools are concerned, you got the education we felt you needed and now the rest is up to you to figure out what to do with it. If you don't succeed, that's your problem. The lender has been sitting back watching and waiting on you to graduate so they can start receiving their money back with interest.

But wait! What if this degree isn't sufficient due to oversaturated market of people with undergraduate degrees and evolving technology? The school will invite you to come back, and they will teach you how to become a "Master" in your area of study and career. Then presumably, you can make even more money.

This is how many college students get entangled in more debt. Imagine a spider's web being set for an unsuspecting insect. The insect can't see the trap, but it's there. Once you get caught, it's difficult to get out. Thus, we have a student loan crisis and millions of students are trapped in student loan bondage as young adults, while living in the land of "the free." This dark side of student loans is something to be mindful of when considering a career that requires a college education. It's easy to get caught up in the student loan trap.

Trade School Benefits

If you are more of a hands-on type of person, going to a trade school may be a better alternative. Learning a specialized skillset can be both rewarding and profitable. There are some specialties that cannot be replaced by a computer. Plumbers, electricians, mechanics, welders, HVAC Technicians, carpenters, painters, roofers, etc., are all specialized skillsets that are both high paying and in high demand. Technology will not be able to replace a roof or diagnose and repair a plumbing issue. There's reliable job security.

Going to trade school is often overlooked because those jobs aren't as glamorous, and the schools don't have the budgets to advertise and market to attract students like some colleges and universities. Consequently, there's a lot of money left on the table in those fields because they go unfilled.

Learning these skills can create opportunities to work for a company or start your own business. For example, as of this writing, the average pay for a Master Electrician in the United States is $34.00 an hour with an average work week of 40 hours, that's $1360.00 per week. That's if you're working for a company. After it's all said and done, that equates to an average of $70,000.00 salary a year and that's not including overtime. The educational requirements are largely based on experience. Of course, there is some classroom knowledge you must obtain, but this education usually will cost significantly less than the four-year college tuition. Also, a two-to-four-year apprenticeship (supervised training) as a beginner (journeyman) electrician will put you closer to becoming a master electrician. Oh, did I mention you're being paid the entire time you're learning as an apprentice? Yeah, while you're being educated in the field, you're also being paid to learn and gain experience.

The same applies with other trade school jobs. There are a lot of opportunities there. We have done a poor job as a society in educating students and young adults about these opportunities. Most of our guidance is steered towards corporate jobs that require a four-year degree or higher. Again, there's nothing wrong with those jobs if that's what you want. For some people these jobs may be a better fit for them.

Let's do some simple math. Let's compare a college student with an apprentice for a skilled labor job. The college student will take out on average $60,000.00 ($15,000.00 a year) in student loans if they go to a public university in state over a 4-year period. In those 4 years, let's assume they were working an entry level job and they have forfeited $30,000.00 a year of earned income they could have been making. This missed income totals $120,000.00 of income they forfeited. Add the $60,000.00 in student loans they have to repay to the $120,000.00 in missed income and now they are negative $180,000.00 the moment they walk across the stage and graduate from college.

The apprentice has paid $5000 for the trade school tuition to learn the basics and within 6 months is now working as an apprentice for a company. As an apprentice, he or she earns $30,000.00 a year while being trained and mentored. After 4 years of training and education, the apprentice has become a licensed Master Electrician. So, they have gained a life skill that will be useful the rest of their life and they have earned $115,000 in the process over the same 4-year timeframe. When they start earning $70,000 a year, they get to keep more of it because they don't have student loans to repay for the next 10-20 years.

This is just an example to help you see or consider alternative options for earning income. After all, the premise of getting an education is to earn income, right? Also, someone may be thinking $70,000.00 a year is not a lot of money. I see your argument and I'll raise my rebuttal with this. Research supports the average millionaire in America never earned over $100,000.00 in annual salary. A single person earning $70,000.00 a year with minimal expenses can easily save and invest over half of their income annually. Over time and with the assistance of compound interest he or she will have built some serious wealth and will be able to live a quality lifestyle. And keep in mind, this is just for one person and not including a spouse. The numbers may vary of course, but in this example, I hope you were able to get the basic idea that some careers and skillsets obtained at a trade school can be profitable and should at least be considered.

Is the Military a good option?

I'm a Navy veteran and I served for almost 6 years. I made a lot of great memories from serving in the Navy and I have no regrets about the time I spent serving. For me, after I graduated from high school, I wasn't interested in attending college. Also, I didn't have anyone in my family steering me in that direction, so it really wasn't an option. Plus, I didn't have the grades needed to get a scholarship or be accepted in a major college.

I knew I had to do something the day of graduation or I was going to be homeless by the time I made it to the parking lot after the ceremony. So, with limited options and exposure, the military seemed like a legitimate option.

I mean, where else can an 18-year-old get a job with full benefits, future college education money, travel to different parts of the world, learn a skill that can be transferred to civilian life, all while getting paid? And those are just some of the basic benefits of serving in the military. Exposure, discipline and structure are intangible benefits that also come with serving in the military. They serve me well even now.

I encourage young teenagers to consider the military as an option. If you serve a basic 4-year term and you want to attend college afterwards, you can still do that. Meanwhile, you've earned some money, gained some exposure to the world, matured a bit, hopefully, and now have someone who will pay for you to go to college. You can have the best of both worlds. 'But Derrick, I will waste four years of my life serving in the military and then going to college.' Well, that's one way to look at it. But consider it like this. You are getting your college education paid for and you will graduate debt free with both military experience and a college degree. You simply made yourself stronger in the job market. Oh, did I mention you were being paid monthly to go to college after serving while the tuition is paid for in full! The Montgomery G.I. Bill pays for tuition and some cost-of-living expenses. This is a pretty sweet option, if you ask me.

'But aren't there risks for serving in the military?' Of course, there are. Some branches are higher risk than others. Military personnel who enlist in the Army and Marine Corp are more likely to come face to face with an enemy combatant and have a higher risk of taking a life or having their life being taken in ground combat. The Air Force and Navy are more long-distance fighters and the potential of ever seeing an enemy up close is rare unless you're in a specialized unit like the Navy Seals.

I chose the Navy largely because they get to travel to more places and the risk for direct exposure to death by combat are significantly reduced. I wasn't looking for adrenaline-filled combat. I experienced enough of that in my neighborhood as a child. Also, when I was a teenager, I watched a TV show called Perry Mason with my grandmother. That show indirectly influenced me to aspire to become a lawyer. Because of that show, I joined the Navy because they had a legal program called JAG. I've always been an advocate for justice and becoming a lawyer was appealing to me. After I graduated, I decided that the Navy was going to pay for it. I went to the recruiter's office to sign up for service the day after I graduated from high school. He quickly sat me in front of a computer to take a test before we could go any further in the process.

The entrance exam or Armed Services Vocational Aptitude Battery (ASVAB) is used to determine an applicant's level of intelligence and problem solving. I scored really high on my military entrance exam. The higher you score on the exam, the more options you have to choose a career path in the military. Because I scored abnormally high, I could have chosen any career path the Navy offered. My recruiter tried to sign me up to be a cryptographer (someone who writes and cracks the encryption code used for sensitive data) for the Navy which was a Top Secret Classified position. But I wanted to be a lawyer, so that's the path I pursued. I never did enroll in the JAG program, but I enjoyed the job I had as a Yeoman and had a great time doing it.

If a high school graduate is considering the military as a viable option, be mindful of some of the job titles in the military. They are not necessarily compatible to what you have in mind as civilians. For example, in the Navy an Engineer is not the Engineer you think of in the office building designing and creating blueprints for buildings and bridges. A Navy Engineer is someone who works in the engine room of the ship making sure the engines operate properly. They are the mechanics of the Navy ship. They are frequently spotted in oily coveralls and have greasy fingers. When you talk to the recruiter and before you sign any paperwork, try to take someone with you who has served in the military to prevent you from signing up for something you will later hate.

Also, if you start the Reserve Officers' Training Corps (ROTC) program while in high school, you will get a head start and your pay will be instantly increased upon joining the military. The school ROTC program can bump you from an E-1 in bootcamp to an E-3. This translates to more money (several hundred dollars more per paycheck) just because you were in ROTC. You are also able to attend a four-year university for free under the ROTC program with an expectation of serving in the military as an Officer upon graduation for a set number of years. Officers in the military are paid more than those who are of the general enlisted ranks.

If you do decide to join the military, here's a little tip to help you navigate your way through bootcamp. IT'S NOT PERSONAL! The instructors are not there to destroy you or ruin your life. They are intentionally trying to break you down mentally to see if they can break you physically. They are simply trying to weed out the weak. But trust me, they spent too much money on you to purposefully try to get rid of you. They need you. You have to learn how to play the game. Put forth your best efforts. Be respectful. Take initiative. Stay positive. You will be fine. It's all mental. Don't allow the tactics to break you. Don't miss out on all the benefits because you caved under a little pressure. Remember, IT'S NEVER PERSONAL!

Now that I've discussed some possible career paths, it's only appropriate that I close this lesson out with what I call "Fire Yourself." I believe this is applicable whichever path you choose whether you are just starting or already working in your desired career.

FIRE YOURSELF!

Once you decide on a career or job, I want you to then immediately Fire Yourself! I did a corporate presentation once for Phillips 66 Gas company a few years ago and I talked to the employees about changing their perspective about their job. The presentation was phenomenal and I believe it is applicable to anyone working a traditional job.

The concept of "Fire Yourself" developed as a closing talking point as I was conducting a presentation for a group of company leaders and several of their employees on personal finances. I told the people working for the company to change how they saw themselves. "FIRE YOURSELF" essentially shifts the way you see yourself and thus how you see the job. It consists of three primary points.

Point ONE: You're not simply an employee.

When you Fire Yourself, you see yourself as an independent contractor providing a service for the organization or company. If you see yourself as just an employee, you will perform like just an employee. You will do the minimum work required to get paid. You will come to work begrudgingly and see it as an **OBLIGATION**. If you don't like the management, you don't mind letting them know. It becomes very obvious that you are somewhat disgruntled.

But when you shift your perspective and see yourself as an independent contractor providing a service, your whole attitude changes. You come to work looking for opportunities to make things better, become more efficient and increase productivity. You don't see work as an obligation, but as an **OPPORTUNITY**. You realize this job is how I'm able to provide for myself and my family. This source of income is what I will use to build my wealth and put myself in a better financial position to free up my time. When you have problems with management, instead of complaining about them, you will see yourself as part of the solution. As an independent contractor you propose ideas that help to *resolve* the issues instead of simply *highlighting* the issues.

Can you see how this mentality can be beneficial? When the company is looking for a new leader or manager, who do you think will rise to the top of their minds? Ooh Ooh! I know this one. It will be the person who treats the job like it's their personal business and appreciates the job. It will be YOU.

I've had the privilege to hear from some of the attendees to this event as well as other speaking events where I shared this insight. The feedback I've received is this shift in mentality has caused many people to find value for their job again, get promotions on the job, be put in charge of different branches to lead and some have even gone on to start their own business as a result of this shift in thinking. Only good will come from this shift in perspective. I promise. So, Fire Yourself!

Point TWO: I don't "HAVE" to go to work. I "GET" to go to work.

Unfortunately, some people see their job as an unforgiving, controlling, abusive dictator in their lives. They act as if they didn't apply for the job, lie a little on the application and ask a friend to put in a good word for them. After the newness of the job wears off, the excitement is gone and the expenses created are consuming most, if not all of the income from the job, it turns into this mean old job and Monday becomes the most dreaded day of the week. You go to work Monday morning looking forward to getting off work Friday evening.

The concept of "Fire Yourself" may help you change your perspective and look internally at yourself and examine your attitude to consider if there are things about you that needs to change? Sure, some things may not be perfect on the job. Those things may not ever change. But you can change your perspective. You can start seeing your job as a tool that will get you out of debt, build your savings cushion, provide shelter for you and your family. You can appreciate what it provides for you. You can do this even if it's not the greatest job. This new perspective will change your attitude about going to work. You will begin to see going to work as a privilege and your opportunity to earn income to build wealth with. Plus, you will very likely be compensated at a higher level because of your approach and attitude. The right people will notice you. I promise.

Point THREE: No one owes you anything. Including a job!

**Caution, some may experience slight turbulence for the next few moments. Please keep your seatbelts fastened.*

One of the things people tend to either forget or just overlook is that no one owes you anything. In case you got distracted, I'm going to say that again. NO ONE OWES YOU ANYTHING! Many people, especially us living in America have become such a spoiled and entitled society. Today everyone wants to be catered to and feels like the rest of the world is supposed to tend to their needs and desires. Well, unfortunately that's not quite how the world works.

If you have this mentality, it's easy to misinterpret your job as your right to have and you can develop this sense of entitlement which causes you to take the job for granted. You fail to take into account that there's no federal mandate for anyone to offer you a job. I'll say it again, *there's no federal mandate to create a job for you to work.* What most have forgotten or perhaps they never understood at all, is that the company you work for is the brainchild of someone who sacrificed a lot of time, money and energy to build. That company is somebody's baby they gave birth to and created an opportunity for you to have employment. They weren't forced by any entity to create this business and neither is there any moral or religious obligation for anyone to create an opportunity for you to work. The very fact that you have a job is a gift. You should learn to treat it as such.

I'm trying to rattle your thinking a bit to get you to see your job/source of income from a different perspective. I'm trying to "Unlock Your Mind."

I'm also trying to get you to appreciate the opportunity you have to earn income and embrace the fact that no one owes you anything. I'm trying to break the mindset and spirit of entitlement if you have it and prevent it if you don't.

I've had the mentality of an entrepreneur ever since I was a teenager picking up empty soda and beer cans along the side of the road to sell to the scrap yard or picking up buckets of pecans to sell to the local market to make some cash. From working in the cotton fields "chopping cotton" (using a garden hoe to cut the weeds from around the cotton in the field so it could fully grow), to washing cars on the weekends, cutting grass, or cleaning office buildings while I was in high school, I've had the mentality of providing a service in exchange for my income. I understood no one owed me anything and if there was anything in life I wanted, I had to work to make it happen. No one else was obligated to provide for me. I concluded that 'if I don't make it happen for myself, it won't happen at all.' That's been my mindset all of my life.

As a result of the service-oriented mindset, all throughout my military career, I advanced and was promoted to the top. I was even extended an opportunity to be accepted into the U.S. Naval Academy (It is a high honor for a ship's Captain to grant a waiver for someone to go from the enlisted ranks to officer candidate school). After attending Annapolis, MD where the Naval Academy is located for a week and learning that in order to take advantage of this once in a lifetime opportunity, I would have to sign an additional 6-year commitment to the Navy, I declined the opportunity. When I served as a Houston police officer, I served and saw myself as a servant of the citizens of Houston. I never received one single complaint. My supervisors all loved me and allowed me to operate without micromanagement. They knew I was going to take care of business. I loved serving and I took great pride in my work. I saw myself as an entrepreneur in a police uniform. I was providing high quality service.

In summary, "firing yourself" is about changing your perspective about the source of your income. Regardless of whose name is at the top of your paycheck, treat your job as if it's your personal business and you're the boss of "YOU Incorporated." If you see yourself as an independent contractor providing a service, you will never have to worry about being unemployed and you will not go lacking. You will attract the attention of all the right people and you will rise to the top of their minds. I hope I've given you some things to consider about some of the life lessons that aren't taught in school.

So far, we've covered some critical topics that were somehow forgotten in school. We've talked about some practical economics and things you should definitely know about money, credit and debt. We've talked a bit about different paths to consider when choosing a career. We've talked about how to make the most of the money we earn from the careers we choose. Now let's talk about the power and potential of sales. The next chapter will be dealing with how to embrace your inner sales. If you're ready, I'm ready. Let's talk about it.

LIFE LESSON THREE

What The Hell...I'm in Sales? Learning to Embrace Selling

Many people are just as intimidated by the thought of having to sell something as they are about giving a public speech. The very thought can be paralyzing for some people. But if we really look at it closely, many of the things we do effortlessly is connected to sales. For example, you having a conversation about dinner and influencing the family to eat spaghetti was an act of selling. One simple definition of selling is to persuade someone to take a particular action. The very fact that you're still reading this book is the result of a sale. Through my writing and sharing of my experiences, I've persuaded you to continue reading the book.

The car you drive and the fuel/electricity you use is the result of a sale. The house you live in is a result of a sale. The clothes on your back, the food you eat, and the bed you sleep in are all the result of a sale. Literally everything you have was the result of someone selling something. So, the key is not to hate selling or fear it, but to harness your inner salesperson and use it to advance you forward in life.

What do I have to sell?

You may say, "Derrick, I'm not in sales and I don't know anything about sales." I would have to respectfully disagree with you. Everyone is in sales, whether they know it or not. Regardless of your job title, you're in sales. Anytime a transaction occurs where two people exchange something of value, a sale just happened. We're all selling even if the thing we're selling is an experience.

For example, a schoolteacher may say, I'm not in sales. I contend, however, that schoolteachers are indeed in sales. Teachers sell information and knowledge to their students. The teacher's job is to sell information so convincingly that students believe the accuracy of the information and subscribe to that information for the rest of their lives – or at least the upcoming exam.

A pastor may say, "I'm not in sales." Again, I respectfully disagree. A pastor is in the business of selling faith. They must convey their faith in a way that non-believers agree to subscribe to the faith. The Pastor/Minister has a joint responsibility with God in this process, but ultimately God affirms with the hearer that which was spoken by the pastor is true. Pastors must convince listeners that God exists and wants to have an active role and relationship with them. And as a result of believing in the faith, the listener will be saved from eternal damnation and the consequences of sin. The pastor must be so compelling in the "sell" that listeners will be willing to modify their behavior, give of their resources, and even distance themselves from friends who have yet to adopt the belief. That's a hard sell!

A recruiter for the military must sell young, high school graduates on the idea they can "Be all that you can be...in the Army" or to become one of "The few...the proud...the Marines." They must convince an 18-year-old kid that the risks of war are mitigated by the reward of a career, college tuition money and the honor of protecting and serving their country against foreign and domestic threats. High school graduates then sign a blank check for several years that allows the government to send them into harm's way if necessary. That's a hard sell.

A young lady who desires to be married may say "I'm not in sales," but I beg to differ. Your essence and your partnership are a product worth having, and the world is no fun without women. You are selling yourself as the most qualified candidate for marriage and you are the obvious choice for your client. You must know your worth. You must be able to demonstrate your value and that you are an asset to the relationship. You must convince a potential husband that you are worth him investing his life and resources to have an exclusive relationship with you. Most assuredly my dear sister, you're in sales! Obviously, the same principle of sales applies if a man is looking for the right partner to marry. He must convince her that he knows how to love her, provide for her physically, spiritually, financially and most definitely emotionally. You Sir are in sales.

The point is, folks, everyone is in sales at some level. As you continue reading the book, I hope you'll begin to see just how much you are involved in sales and harness the power to represent yourself well.

Harness your influence for profits

The way we sell products today has drastically changed from 50 years ago. There are very few door-to-door salesmen anymore. Today, most sales take place in cyberspace or by word-of-mouth referrals, which makes it much easier for anyone to profit from sales compared to older models of sales. Today we have a growing number of social media "influencers" who are using their platform to earn six figure incomes by selling or advertising products to their followers.

One of the key success factors to being a salesperson is influence. To be a great salesperson, you must have the ability to influence people to make a decision to take a corresponding action. Your ability to influence people is built on trust. People do business with individuals or companies/brands they know, like and trust. Trust provides the foundation for credibility and the more credible you are, the more influence you stand to gain.

The next thing you need is a product or service that's in demand. Demand is usually based on a need, desire or perceived opportunity. Once you have identified the needs and or desires of people, you essentially have to present your solution to them and offer it at a price they are willing to pay. That's all there is to sales.

Don't be afraid of rejection. It's not personal.

For some reason, the vast majority of people are terrified of sales or a job as a direct salesperson. I wonder why? I mean sales is one of the highest paying careers and offers the greatest amount of freedom. Are you afraid of a sales position? Why do you think many people are intimidated by sales?

Perhaps the primary reason so many people are intimidated by the thought of selling is because of the underlying fear of rejection. Let's face it, the fear of rejection is a powerful and paralyzing emotion. What I've learned as a result of being in sales for nearly half of my life as a realtor and author is that rejection is almost never personal when it comes to sales. But it sure does feel personal.

Trust me I know the feeling all too well. In my experience, there are few things more painful emotionally than someone saying "no!" to a proposition or sale. That "no" can sting and seemingly last forever.

But I can assure you, it's not personal. Here are some potential reasons why people may reject your offer. The first reason might be that they don't have or see a need for the product or service you are offering. The second potential reason is they don't have the money to spend on your product/service or the authorization to do so (if you're selling to a company). A third potential reason for someone rejecting your offer or product is that there is a better product or service available at a better price somewhere else.

If you notice, the three most likely reasons for someone rejecting your product or service have absolutely nothing to do with the salesperson as an individual. It's about where the person is and what they are able to do. Keeping this in mind, a great salesperson expects and prepares for rejection. That's what makes them great. Even if the sale is not completed, a great salesperson is able to detach themselves personally from the transaction and move on to the next potential customer. Unfortunately, because of a fear of rejection, people may forfeit potentially high-earning incomes in sales. Instead of earning a sizable income, they end up "selling themselves short." Go figure.

Change your perspective about sales.

Unfortunately, when people hear sales, they cringe and almost instantly think of a poorly dressed, sleezy, used car salesman or worse – a well-dressed salesman who doesn't seem to comprehend the word no trying to sell them a timeshare. And consequently, bad salesmen have given the sales profession a bad name. Trust me, if all salesmen were like that, I wouldn't even mention sales as an important life skill to possess.

But consider this. When you think of sales, perhaps a better perspective would be to think of it as helping others by providing a needed or desired service. For example, think of a pharmaceutical sales representative. These are the people who work for pharmaceutical companies and their role is to sell doctors on the use of medications to help treat their patients. If the doctor prescribes the drugs to their patients and the drugs alleviate the pain of patients who are suffering, did the pharmaceutical rep make a sale or did they help that patient alleviate his/her pain. The salesperson simply provided a solution to the doctor who then met the goal of helping their patient feel better.

When you look at yourself as someone who has a solution for someone else's problems, then what you're doing is not really sales anymore. You are offering a solution and there's nothing wrong with being compensated for solving a problem and offering a solution to help someone else. That's an honorable and a noble thing to do. It's part of doing business. Embedded in the motives of a great salesperson is the spirit of providing excellent service. Let's talk a bit about service shall we.

Serving is not a curse word. It's a privilege.

What's the first thought that comes to your mind when you hear the word 'servant' or 'service?' Is it a janitor, room service, bellhop, waiter/waitress, or some other profession? Sometimes, the notion of serving or being a servant invokes negative reactions for people. Perhaps it's because some people feel as if they should be the ones being served, or maybe they view those doing the serving as less than themselves.

Regardless of how people feel about the notion of serving, the reality is, to be great in business and in life, you must provide great service. I am convinced, one of the most important skillsets we can possess is that of providing service to others. The concept of serving applies whether you're serving as a spouse, a server in a food establishment, a pastor, a business owner, entertainer or commission-based sales professionals.

We're all serving someone. Personally, I place a very high value on receiving great service and an even greater value on providing great service to others. However, great service is slowly becoming a lost art these days. Regardless of where you are in the world, I'd be willing to bet you the businesses providing great service is significantly more profitable than their competition. Why? Because people place a high value on good service and they will support, patronize and reward those who provide it.

There's a popular fast-food chain in America that only sells chicken. Not gourmet chicken. Just pressure cooked lightly breaded chicken. They only provide a handful of options to eat chicken. Either in sandwich form, nuggets, tenders or on a salad. That's all they sell. But wait, is that all they sell? Just chicken?

No! They are selling a great experience. They are selling consistency. They are selling a personalized and catered experience when they ask for your name before taking your order. They are selling SERVICE. They frequently greet you in the drive through line with "how can I serve you today?" They ask "may I have a name for the order?" Finally, the last thing you hear from them is "it was my pleasure." From the time they open for business until the time they close, there are usually lines of cars buying their chicken. Or are they buying their SERVICE?

When you build your brand around providing great service, people will be more inclined to support you. For example, I started a lawn business with my son at the age of 12 so he could learn how to earn his own money and also to keep him from asking me for money all the time. I invested this time and labor in him because I wanted to teach him several things about money, and this was the best way to do it at a young age. He cuts the grass and I do all the fine trimming of the edges. During our time working together, I try to teach him life lessons and business principles that will prepare him for understanding the value of hard work and entrepreneurship. One of the main lessons I teach him is that of providing excellent service. In the spirit of excellence, I make him go back over a yard if it's not cut evenly or if he missed a spot. I make him blow the grass or leaves off the driveway until they are all gone. I make him pay attention to the smallest details. Why? I want him to understand that people will compensate you well for providing great service. But if they don't like your service, they have options to pay someone else who provides a better service. I am trying to instill in him the importance of doing things with a spirit of excellence – even the small things – and to take pride in providing great service. I want him to know when he places a high value on providing great service to others, doors and opportunities can open for him in the future.

I hope this life lesson challenged you to reexamine your perspective on sales and service. The reality is, some of the most successful people in life are the ones who understand and fully embrace the role of being a great salesman while simultaneously providing great service to the people they have as customers.

Now that we've talked a bit about sales, let's discuss the importance of branding yourself. Did you know you had a brand? Come on over and let's talk about it.

LIFE LESSON FOUR

Your Personal Brand Awareness

What is a brand? One technical definition of a brand is "an intangible marketing concept that helps people identify companies, products and individuals." My practical definition for the purpose of this writing can be defined as "*what an individual, company or product is known for.*" When it comes to success in life, your personal brand, or how you present yourself, is particularly important. Your personal brand consists of characteristics, personality, behaviors or other intangible attributes that people associate with you.

What's your brand? What are you known for? When people think of you, what thoughts do you think come to mind? A significant part of your ability to advance in life hinges on your personal brand, or the credibility of your word, the quality of service you provide, and your sense of integrity and commitment to ethical practice. Your personal brand is so important that it affects your ability to achieve your dreams, goals, aspirations. Given the importance of your personal brand, let's take a moment to talk about it.

You're sending a message...But what are you saying?

For as long as we have existed, humans have made observations and assessments of life, people and situations based on how we see it with our eyes and perceive it with our minds. Much of how we see is based on our personal experiences. We learn how to make visual observations and assessments early on.

If you don't mind, please grant me a few liberties here to share from my religious beliefs for a moment. This is to help further illustrate the point. According to the Bible in the book of Genesis Chapter 2 verse 7, in the Creation narrative, Adam was the first human being and he was all alone (Genesis 2:18).

He saw with his eyes that there was no one else like him. There were animals who had compatible or similar animals. But Adam didn't have anyone like him to relate to (Genesis 2:20). God realized this and immediately fixed the problem. God said to Himself, "it is not good for man to be alone." God put Adam to sleep and when he awakened God had created another human being – a female version of man (Genesis 2:21-25). Instantly, Adam visually observed the new person and saw the distinction between himself and the new one and he called her "womb-man" or man with a womb. He perceived she was different from him and the way she presented herself made him desire her. What he saw with his eyes communicated to him that he was no longer alone. He had someone compatible to him to communicate with. He had someone he could be intimate with. In Genesis 2:24 Adam said, "for this reason shall a man leave his father and mother and cling to his wife." He didn't even have a father or mother. But he knew he liked what he saw and was willing to forsake all others for her. I'm just going to go out on a limb here and say Eve must have been a fine specimen of a woman. She had my man Adam hooked. Surely Adam didn't know the drama she would bring into his life. But that's not the point. Moving right along.

What was the point of that story? I wanted to show you that as far back as the very beginning of creation, we humans learned to assess people by what we see before we assess them by what they know or say. We communicate more with our appearance than you may realize.

Visual communication is not necessarily a bad thing. Visual assessments are a useful tool for survival. We learn to assess danger or what we perceive to be dangerous and make the appropriate decisions in order to protect ourselves based on what we see. We learn to identify friends from foes based on our visual assessment of them. What we see with our eyes sends a message to our brains well before a single word has been spoken. This is helpful and necessary for our survival.

What do you see?

We have the unique ability to communicate through multiple senses. The five senses we all learned about in school are sight, sound, touch, taste and smell. However, one of the most commonly used forms of communications is our sight. Wait, one would think it would be through talking. Right? No. Studies show the majority of what we convey to others is non-verbal. Some examples of non-verbal communication are our body movement, facial expression, tone of voice, eye contact, hand gestures, attire, demeanor, and posture. These are just a few.

Dr. Albert Mehrabian, one of the leading researchers on non-verbal communication, devised a formula to describe how the mind determines or interprets meaning. He concluded that the interpretation of a message is 7 percent verbal, 38% vocal and 55% visual. One might ask, what's the difference in verbal and vocal? Great question. Verbal communication refers to the actual words spoken in the communication. Vocal is the tone, volume, pace, accent interference, etc. A simpler understanding is verbal is "WHAT" you said and vocal is "HOW" you said it. So, only 7% of communication is what you said and 38% is how you said it and the rest was observed visually through your body language. The conclusion was that 93% of communication is nonverbal or unspoken in nature. All this really means is ***people will make assessments and decisions about you before you ever open your mouth.***

Your life is a show and people are watching.

How you "show up" matters in life. If you dress like a gangster, people may treat you like one. Generally, people are afraid of gangsters and so you may be treated accordingly. So, don't be surprised if people avoid you or clutch their purse around you. You told them to fear you with how you presented yourself. If you dress in slacks or a suit, people may see you from afar and generally make positive assessments about you. If you dress in very revealing attire, people may treat you differently than a lady in modest clothing. If you dress in a uniform, people will generally treat you with respect and give deference to your authority simply because of the uniform.

Your appearance matters. For some reason, my teenage son wants a tattoo and he asked me if he could get dreadlocks. I said absolutely not! I know there's nothing inherently wrong with either of those, but the message it sends is viewed negatively by the majority of society and thus it may speak for him well before he opens his mouth. I unfortunately have to discourage him from wearing certain hairstyles and clothing as a young black male. Being a former police officer, I know all too well how profiling works. There are clues, signs, patterns of behavior, and attire that all communicate specific messages to police officers. Those visual messages help to create what they call profiles (behavioral characteristics). Profiling is a terrible reality, but it is the reality and I can't ignore it.

People naturally and instinctively pre-judge others based on what they see. We all do it unconsciously and this tendency is actually called unconscious bias. As I write this book, I'm in a small town called Campbellsville, Kentucky. It's a very small farm town. I haven't seen many people who look like me since I've been here. I made many observations and assessments about the people here. A few times I felt uncomfortable based on my past experiences, the stereotypes I held, even the strong accent they had. However, after several encounters with some of the people, I quickly had to check my biases and I realized I was doing to them exactly what I hate being done to me. I prejudged them purely on how they looked instead of how they were. They were as nice as can be to me. I had to literally re-adjust my perspective of them. I think I was more shocked at how well they treated me. Sometimes what we see with our eyes can be deceiving and we can have the wrong interpretation. This is one of those times. I share this just to let you know we all have biases and we all pre-judge others by what we see with our eyes before we get to know the person or situation.

Being aware of this tendency gives you an advantage over many others. Being mindful of bias helps you regulate how you present yourself, especially in public. The message you send by way of your attire, demeanor, timeliness, tone of voice, body language, and others all are sending messages that inform people's impression of you. If you want to make the kind of impressions that help open doors of opportunity, it is important to be intentional about the message you're sending as part of your personal brand. We can miss many opportunities in life by how we present ourselves and how others perceive us based on what they see.

Speak LIFE into your BRAND.

There are some beliefs that suggest repeating affirmations to yourself daily can positively impact one's life. An affirmation is a positive encouraging phrase or statement you read aloud to yourself frequently as a way of embedding it into your brain and belief system until you manifest the desired behavior or outcome. I imagine if you told yourself daily "I am an intelligent, compassionate, kind, thoughtful, giving, considerate, loving, fun person," over time your brain will believe it and you will act on those beliefs. I do know for a fact that our brain will generally get in agreement with what we tell it to believe.

How does Timeliness affect your BRAND?

Timeliness, or punctuality, speaks volumes about our personal brand. We were most likely introduced to the concept of time during childhood when our parents woke us up early, so we could catch the bus on time for school. In school, there were structured times for everything. The time was marked with a loud bell which was our indication that it was time to start one thing and stop another. The bell indicated to everyone that school had started and everyone should be in their designated classrooms. The bell was the timekeeper of the day and we governed ourselves by it. Well, in school, if you were late to class, you would get a tardy slip and your teacher would likely ask you "why are you late to my class?" to which you would give some explanation or excuse.

The more tardy slips you accumulate, the more severe the consequences for being late became – starting with a warning, moving to ISS (IN SCHOOL SUSPENSION) which was followed by a phone call to your parents and ultimately, school suspension. If none of these penalties worked and motivated you to be on time to class, the school would then start to penalize your parents by assessing them with a fine in an attempt to help the student understand the importance of getting to class on time.

Unfortunately, patterns of tardiness that are developed early in life rarely go away as we become adults unless there is an intentional intervention. While some behaviors change as we age, most of them don't. If you put forth little effort in school, there's a good chance you will put forth little effort in life. If you had a nonchalant attitude about timeliness as a teenager, there's a high probability that you may have that same approach as an adult. Not always, but there is a high probability that this will happen.

Why are we talking about this? Because unlike the classroom, there are more harsh consequences for your tardiness in the real world than there are in school. Companies will terminate your employment for tardiness. The company you work for is paying you to be there on time to perform your duties. No one is interested in hearing your excuses about why you were late- particularly if you have a non-emergency related habit of showing up late for work. As discussed earlier, no one owes you a job. Thus, it would be to your advantage to show up on time and do what is required of you if you want to continue receiving a paycheck.

One of the most common reasons given for why an employee was terminated is because they were chronically late for work. Rather than learn from this experience and commit to timeliness in the future, some people blame their termination on the boss and accuse their boss of "trippin'" or "hating on them". No silly rabbit, you were terminated because you did not respect time. Your employer hired you to work a set number of hours in order to produce a set amount of goods and services per workday. Whenever you show up late, you violate your agreement and you shortchange the company on the amount of productivity that can be expected from you. Violation of timeliness is a violation of boundaries, and a violation of boundaries is a reflection of your credibility and your personal brand. While you may not suffer extreme consequences in school, the real world may not be as forgiving.

Of course, I understand that life happens to all of us and there are times when we may be understandably late. But this should not be the norm. It should be so rare, that if or when you are late, people are shocked by it because this type of behavior is not characteristic of you. Remember we're still talking about your brand and how people perceive you.

ALL TIMES MATTER.

One of my pet peeves is being late for an event, meeting or function. I hate it. I set my schedule to ensure I'm at the appointed place at the appointed time. Because I know how I feel when people don't respect my time, I intentionally adjust my life to ensure I respect other people's time.

Anyone who violates my time has instantly annoyed me, and I begin making negative assessments about them with every minute that goes past the time we were supposed to start or end. This also applies for events that are scheduled to start at a certain time and end at a certain time. I hate "CP TIME" (google it). 'But that's mean.' No! What's mean is the person's lack of consideration for my time and other events I may have in place that are time sensitive. What's mean is your lack of intentionality of adhering to the schedule we agreed to. Your lateness creates a cascading effect that may result in me having to adjust my schedule. Your lateness has forced me to have to a make a decision to leave before our encounter is completed or be late to my next appointment, thereby violating their time. When it comes to your personal brand as a person, a parent, an employee, an entrepreneur, etc. where people are depending on you, lack of timeliness is unacceptable.

Let's look at an example. Imagine you had an appointment with your barber at 10:00 am, and it usually takes 30 minutes for the haircut. Based on that timeframe, you set an appointment for a job interview at 12:00 noon. Your job interview is 30 minutes away from your barber so you build in 90 minutes of cushion time to account for traffic. If all goes well, you plan to leave the barber shop at 10:30 on your way to your job interview. You've got a fresh haircut so you're looking good and feeling good. Ideally, you should arrive at the job interview by 11:00-11:15 with plenty of time to find the building, calm your nerves, get your mind right for the 12:00 noon interview. Because you don't want your first impression to the interviewers to reflect that you don't value timeliness, you adjust your life accordingly. However, you arrive at the barber shop at 10:00 am and your barber or stylist doesn't get there until 11:15. You've been waiting for an hour and 15 minutes for them. Now, not only have you wasted 75 minutes of your life, but you can't get your haircut or you will be late to the interview. And all your barber can say is I'm sorry, I overslept. Use your imagination and put yourself in the customers shoes. How would you feel?

How much does my time negligence cost?

Caution: Some may experience a bit of turbulence.

As a real estate investor, I own several rental properties. I occasionally use contractors for a job that I don't know how to do or don't want to do. If they agree to meet with me at 10:00 am, I'm there at 9:50 am waiting. If they have not arrived by 10:01, I'm starting to make assessments about their credibility. If I have not heard anything from them with an updated time of arrival and brief explanation for why they are running behind by 10:25, I will leave. They just lost the job and any future jobs. Why? Because what being late communicates to me is they don't value my time. Not communicating within the 25 minutes you were late also says they don't respect me enough to let me know they will not be there at the agreed upon time. It also says to me that they may not complete the job on time and on schedule which could lead to more frustration. It says I can't trust them to keep their word. I will think twice about referring them to a friend, client or relative because I can't trust them to be on time. This may sound rather harsh, or rigid, but trust me a paying customer has expectations of you respecting their time. These are things perhaps no one has ever vocalized to you before, but many people feel this way about their time.

Here's the thing about these scenarios, I'm the type of person that may not say anything to them directly, but I will not likely use them again for future business. I will speak by withholding my resources. Again, remember I said people are always making assessments about you and how you show up. Remember I said communication is largely non-verbal. We are still talking about our personal brand. The barber's or contractor's non-verbal communication was that they don't respect or value my time, my schedule or me as a paying customer. Therefore, I treat them accordingly. I will take my money and give it to someone who respects my time.

Now do you see how timeliness has an impact on you? Can you see how your being late can speak on your behalf louder than the words that you *never* spoke? Do you see how timeliness impacts your economics? I hope you are starting to see how important timeliness is to your economics.

Take a moment though to do a quick self-evaluation of yourself and how you treat time. Are you punctual? Would others consider you punctual? If you have plans with your spouse or friends, do they anticipate and expect you to be late? Is your value for being on time high (very important), medium (sort of important) or low (not important)? Can you see how important timeliness is or can be for others? Can you see how others may perceive you and make negative assessments about you if you're frequently late. This is not a judgment. I'm writing this to help you see how and why this is important. And also, the negative consequences that could either follow or be avoided. Please be considerate of other peoples' time. I beg of you.

BONUS: BE CONSIDERATE AND DON'T MAKE PEOPLE WAIT FOR YOU.

Also, since we're on the subject of time. If someone is picking you up and they tell you what time to be ready. Please be there ready and waiting for them. It is very inconsiderate to have someone go out of the way to help you, pick you up and you not be on time. The older I get, the less tolerance I have for people who ask me for a ride but are not ready when I arrive. Again, I have planned my life and schedule ahead of time, so I made accommodations for picking you up. However, when you are not ready upon my arrival, you impact my schedule. Your delay was not factored into my planning. By not being ready you are telling me to not offer you a ride again because you can't prioritize your time and you have little value or consideration for my time. If someone is helping you, make it a pleasant experience. Don't make them regret helping you.

Repairing a damaged brand.

So, what can you do to repair your brand? That's a great question. The simple answer is to change your behavior. Anything short of behavior modification seems like artificial repentance, which is temporary remorse about negative consequences without any substantive actions that suggest you are trying to change.

If you have created a context where people see you a certain way, or you have established a pattern of behavior that is negatively impacting you, you must demonstrate that you are now aware of the issue and you fully acknowledge how the issue or concern has shaped how you are perceived. But you can't stop there. Awareness is step one. But awareness alone is useless. You must take the necessary steps to correct the behavior and even communicate to others your intentions. For example, if you have been habitually late to work, events, functions, etc., start by being extra early. Be intentional about making sure you are mindful of your time and the time of others. By engaging in clear change actions, you can slowly rebuild trust and credibility with people. The process of rebuilding trust and credibility may take some time, but your demonstration of consistency when it comes to timeliness can do wonders in shaping how people see and relate to you.

Is there more that I need to do? Nope. Allowing your changed behavior enough time to replace the brand you once had with the new and improved version is the main thing you need do to repair a damaged brand. The good news is that with time, you can re-brand yourself.

LIFE LESSON FIVE

Traps to Avoid...That Can Lead to Poverty

What comes to your mind when you think of a trap? The very first thought I have is of a rat trap. I remember the time when my daughter told me she saw a rat in the house. Usually, she screams like her life is being taken when she sees the smallest little bug in the house. However, on this occasion she didn't scream. Since her reaction was so calm, I initially thought she may have been playing about seeing a rat. Eventually, she convinced me that she really did see a rat in the house, and she provided a pretty impressive description of the suspect. As any good father would do, I had to protect my daughter from this menacing rat. I had to figure out how to locate the rat, capture it, and then get it out of the house. I did a brief search online and discovered that rats and mice like nuts and grains and they typically come out at night to eat.

Armed with the knowledge of what attracts rats and how they operate, I developed a plan to capture the rat. I bought some sticky glue pads and placed them around the house near the area where my daughter said she saw the rat. I put a mixed variety of nuts on the glue pads to attract them. I figured I would give them options to choose from since this would be their last meal in my home. The trap was set. The only thing I could do now was wait.

So, I went to sleep, unsure of what would happen.

As fate would have it, my plan worked! I was awakened at 4am the next morning by my wife screaming as though someone had broken into the house. She screamed in total panic "what's that noise!" "It's in the living room...it's in the living room!" Unsure of who or what exactly was in the living room, I quickly got out of bed, grabbed my gun and proceeded to go investigate. By then, I'd heard the noise too and I was able to determine that the intruder was not a person, so I put my gun away. The sound I heard was nothing like anything I had heard before. I have tile floors in my home, so whatever "it" was woke us up as a result of scurrying across the floor. I finally determined "it" was the rat. The trap had worked! I heard the plastic glue trap being drug across the tile floors and the frantic whimpers of the trapped rat.

Now what? I knew how to deal with a human intruder. But a trapped rat! I was just as scared as she was. The screams from my wife eventually woke up everyone else in the house except my daughter. Somehow, she slept through the entire ordeal.

As I came out of my bedroom into the living room, we could hear the rat scurrying around, but it was still dark, and we didn't know exactly where it was. After a few minutes passed, all the lights were now on, a broom was in my hands and my adrenaline was pumping. I will admit, I was mildly scared, but in a manly kind of way. I finally was able to isolate the sound and I located it. The rat had somehow climbed onto the wood frame of the sofa from underneath it. After a whole 20-minute ordeal, my son and I were finally able to trap, capture and dispose of the rat.

Why did I tell you that story? Pay close attention. I wanted you to see how my intentional and deliberate efforts to trap and capture the rat were a success. I appealed to its appetite to lure it into captivity. I studied what it liked and I developed a plan to safely remove the rat from my home. Similar to what I did to capture the rat, there are traps set for us that are intended to lure us into more debt, lead to self-destructive behaviors, cause us to live above our means, and keep us in poverty.

Some of the traps are self-inflicted. Some of them are strategically put in place by people who have studied what your appetites are, when you are most likely to consume the things you like, and how to strategically present them to you. They know you can't resist the temptation, so they put the traps in place and simply wait for you to take the bait. Then BOOM! Gotcha! You're stuck in something and can't get out of it. The end results are usually not favorable.

I will give you a few examples of traps that are dangerous and encourage you to avoid them if possible. I know they are tempting and they may appeal to your senses. But remember my buddy the rat. I used what it liked and its' own appetite to lure it into my trap, ultimately to destroy it. That's how many of these traps are set up. The things we will discuss are topics that were not discussed in school, but being aware of these dangers is essential to our ability to function holistically in society. Are you ready? Cool. Let's talk about it.

Trap #1: Keeping up with the Joneses.

If we're honest, we all suffer a bit from wanting to keep up with what others are doing. Some refer to it as "keeping up with the Joneses." This idiom refers to comparing oneself to your neighbors or using your neighbors as the benchmark for social class, financial status or the accumulation of material goods. It highlights the human tendency to want what others have, particularly when it comes to images of success. With the introduction of social media, social platforms have magnified the desire to keep up with the Joneses because we are constantly exposed to what appears to be a successful life – at least online.

In some cases, it isn't necessarily a bad thing to engage in comparisons – particularly when the comparisons are positive and drive us to work harder and to accomplish more in our lives. Positive comparisons can help us stretch beyond our current limitations, become better people, and unlock our minds to find ways to get some of the things we desire. Seeing others with something we want indirectly says we too can have it and it suggests it's possible to obtain it. And for the record, I'm not talking about seeing someone else's husband or wife and saying I can have them too. Absolutely not! Lol.

All jokes aside, this positive influence can be good in the right context. However more often than not, this desire or appetite to keep up with others drives us in negative ways. It can create a never-ending cycle of wanting more and more and more and more! It can foster a super competitive nature that can become obsessive and possessive, which only serves to bring out the worst parts of our personality.

Trying to keep up with others can cause you to spend money you don't have in order to convey a lifestyle that you really can't afford. Comparisons can keep you broke as you try to impress others. BREAKING NEWS!!! THE JONESES ARE BROKE!!! Keep in mind, the term "broke" is relative to the individual. So, when I say they are broke, I don't mean literally that they don't have any money. However, according to statistics, 7 out of 10 people are living paycheck to paycheck. That's 70 percent of the people you know. Think about ten of your friends. Then count seven of them and they may be secretly living from paycheck to paycheck. Some of them have larger paychecks, which means they may appear to be doing better. They have bigger toys to play with, but most of the toys and items we see are financed and payments are being made on them. One or two missed payments on their toys will indicate who the real "owners" are when they are repossessed.

This trap of keeping up with the Joneses will have you perpetually trying to obtain more stuff because someone else has it. It can create this insatiable appetite for more and more and more wherein you'll never be satisfied. As a result, you may struggle financially because the money you could have been saving, investing, growing and stowing away was spent buying crap you didn't need just to impress people you don't know and may not even like. Keeping up with the Joneses can lead you to poverty.

What I've discovered is just because people have nice things, go on nice vacations and take great pictures of their lifestyles to post on social media, does not always mean that what they are representing is their reality. In fact, for most people what you see is likely a façade – *an outward appearance that is maintained to conceal a less pleasant reality.* To the person on the outside looking in, their lifestyles are desirable. But the truth is, their realities are not as glamorous as they look.

Here's an example of how our perspective can cause us to want what others have while taking for granted what we already have. In 2021 I traveled to Ghana, Africa seeking potential opportunities to invest in some real estate. The trip helped me realize something fascinating about human perception and desire to have what others have. Here I was traveling out of America looking for opportunities in Ghana, Africa. But when I got there, many of the people I met hated living there and wished they could come and live in America. This realization helped me to see how we all have a desire for something we don't have and many times we don't appreciate and value what we do have because of our appetite for something else.

In my mind, I was willing to trade the opportunities I had in America to prosper, while working tirelessly to maintain a lifestyle of constantly buying stuff, in exchange for the simplicity of life and low cost of living in Ghana, as I perceived it. They were willing to exchange the simplicity of life and the low cost of living for the opportunity to work long hours, earn a high income, and live the American dream as they perceived it. I wanted what they had and they wanted what I had.

If we're not intentional, we can find ourselves unsatisfied with our lives because we are too enamored with the lives of others. This trap can be costly, so try to avoid it. Now, let's discuss the next trap.

Trap #2: THE COMPARISON TRAP

Truth is, there will always be someone out there who has more than you. Someone will always have a bigger house, nicer car, faster boat, nicer shoes, better body, prettier wife, more attractive husband, fancier clothes, bigger church, more followers, etc. The sooner you realize this and accept this, the sooner you can start to live a life fulfilling and satisfying for you. You can actually enjoy what you have and the things God has blessed you with. You can be proud of the things you've achieved and accomplished in life without the cloud of unappreciation that comes with comparing yourself to others. The truth of the matter is we don't know what other people had to do to obtain the things they have. We don't know the sacrifice they had to endure to get what they have. We usually see the end results, but we rarely see the process it took to get there.

In the Bible, we are warned in Exodus 20:17 not to covet (yearn to possess) your neighbor's house, wife, servants, ox, donkey or anything that is your neighbor's. This was one of the Ten Commandments of God. By avoiding this trap, you will save yourself from a lot of emotional stress, disappointment, and feelings of inadequacy. Most importantly you will save a lot of money that you can use for something more meaningful to you.

Also remember, no one has it all together, regardless of how much money they have. Rich people have problems just like poor people. The person who is poor financially may struggle to make ends meet, but are rich in love, community, companionship, and are genuinely happy with life. But he or she may feel as if they would be more fulfilled if they had more money. While on the other hand, the person rich financially doesn't have a financial need that can't be met, yet they would long to have genuine friends that aren't after their money, loving relationships with people they can trust, a community of friends and family that supports them with no hidden agenda. When we fall into the trap of comparisons, we overlook what we have because we're too busy looking at what someone else has.

Another dangerous comparison made far too often is with men and women who secretly and quietly compare their body parts, shapes, features, etc. to others. Listen, all this does is create internal emotional distress that remains confidential, but haunts our thoughts. There are no benefits to this comparison. There's absolutely nothing you can do to change your body build with the exception of weight management or some type of expensive surgery. You have what you have. Learn how to make the best of it.

Learn to love you the way you were created. When you love you, it's much easier for others to love you. If you don't love you and you are always displeased with you, how can you possibly expect someone else who's secretly dealing with their own insecurities to fully love and appreciate you, if all they hear is you talking down about you? It's nearly impossible. You are enough just as you are. Be your best self and allow others to enjoy your uniqueness.

Trap #3: A Faulty Belief System

In my first book, Unlock Your Mind...Unlock Your Money, I talked about how our beliefs and mentality impact and shape our lives. I described how those beliefs also impact our economics. Think about it – most of the things you see in existence today are the result of someone acting on a thought that they believed in enough to put in the work to make it a reality, including this very book. I genuinely believe I have a message that can help millions of people just like you.

What you choose to believe impacts and influences your life in many ways. But what happens when your beliefs are built on faulty premises or truths? What happens when you passionately believe in something, but you are passionately wrong? This trap can cause you to act or not act based on bad data. Let's talk about it.

Having bad data that has created a faulty belief system can lead you straight into a trap that can be difficult to escape. One such trap is believing you are always right and not allowing yourself to be wrong or feeling as if your way is the only way. This trap leads to another trap which is being unwilling to change or compromise your position...for the sake of your beliefs. Once you get inside this trap, it becomes like a maze and it's hard to find your way out without asking some questions. But many people are so passionate about what they believe, it's difficult at times to see the need for help. Many of the treasured beliefs were inherited or passed down to them and they don't even know the origins of the beliefs. So, how do you escape those types of traps?

Here's one solution that can help you navigate your way out of this trap. Learn to ask the question Why. Here's a classic example of why asking the question why can stop generational foolishness. As the story goes, a young lady was preparing to cook ham for thanksgiving dinner for the first time. Her husband saw her cutting the ends off the ham before putting it in the oven to bake. So out of curiosity, he asked her "sweetie why did you cut a perfectly good piece of ham off and throw it away?" She replied, "I don't know, that's how my mom did it." So, the husband, now perplexed, he decides to call his mother-in-law to inquire about why she cut the ends of the ham off. To his surprise, she had a similar response. "That's how my mom did it when I was growing up." Now even more confused, he decides to call his wife's grandmother. Granny, I'm trying to figure out what's the reason for cutting the ends off the ham. My wife just threw out one third of the ham for no apparent reason, so can you explain this to me? After a slight sarcastic chuckle, she answered "Baby, I don't know why they do it, but I cut the ends off my hams because I didn't have a pan large enough to hold it. I cut off the ends so it would fit in my pan." The moral of the story is sometimes we perpetuate customs and beliefs out of traditions that we never stopped to question. We never stopped to ask WHY. Thus, we develop and perpetuate a faulty belief system.

Here's how a faulty belief system can affect you financially and lead you to poverty. You "believe" you have a chance at winning the lottery one day, if you keep playing, so you spend $20 a week buying lotto tickets, not realizing you're wasting over $1000 annually that could have been invested or at best saved. Imagine doing this for your entire 20-year work life. Can you see how this faulty belief can cause you to forfeit building wealth and actually be keeping you impoverished?

Here's another big one. You believe you will always have a check coming in because you have a "secure job." Remember earlier when I transitioned out of the Navy and was broke? I fell into the trap of thinking I will always have a paycheck. Based on this belief, you fail to prioritize saving money, because after all you will be paid again in two weeks. Right? If you are convinced you will "always" have a secure source of income, you don't prepare for the day when you may not have that source of income. You don't account for risk. You don't account for company downsizing, company mergers, company relevance to the market, etc. You don't account for injuries. You don't account for policy changes that impact your income. You don't account for technological advancements that could make your job irrelevant one day. But because you have a faulty belief, you continue going through life as if you are financially invincible and will always have a steady paycheck.

This belief can make us lazy and lethargic with our savings goals. It can cause us to become comfortable with taking on a lot of consumer debt. Why? Because we believe we can afford it. It can cause us to purchase things we don't need and that don't fit within our already tight budget. When we maintain a belief that we'll always have job security, or we can gamble our way to wealth, we can easily be lured into a slow financial death. This is a dangerous trap you should avoid.

Trap #4: The Deception of Intoxication

Let's face it. Life can be hard. Life can present us with complicated situations, events and circumstances that can be downright hurtful. Sometimes the complications of life are self-inflicted and other times they are caused by someone else. We didn't ask for the pain, yet the pain showed up without consulting with us about it. There are also times when life feels fulfilling, meaningful and purposeful. We have moments of excitement when things are going well for us, and we feel optimistic about life and the direction our future is going. We achieve major milestones and accomplishments that are worth celebrating.

If you live long enough, you will experience both the highs and lows of life. While the highs feel good, the lows can feel emotionally overwhelming and are hard to cope with. Because the lows are guaranteed, it's important to find healthy ways to cope with life's difficulties in a way that builds resilience. When we don't have healthy coping strategies, we may find ourselves turning to unhealthy coping strategies, including the use of alcohol or substances as a way to block out emotional pain. I'm not sure when the first alcoholic beverage was created. However, I recall the first-time hearing about it in the Bible was in the book of Genesis chapter 9:20. Noah was a man of God who built an ark as instructed by God. According to the narrative, it rained and God destroyed an entire generation of people by a flood because of their wickedness. Noah and his family were the only ones to survive the flood. After the flood, Noah got drunk and he was found in his tent laid out butt naked and wasted. Undoubtedly after experiencing such a horrific event and witnessing massive human casualties, I imagine he used alcohol to help manage the pain and come to grips with the devastation that followed the flood. He may have felt guilty and questioned whether or not he tried hard enough to warn people. Regardless of the reason for his emotional pain, it is probably safe to say that Noah had a lot going on in his head and he was looking for some type of relief. So, he drank himself to sleep.

Alcohol and drugs can provide a sense of pleasure and euphoria. At the same time, alcohol and drugs can be used to numb emotional pain and provide a temporary escape from the thoughts in your mind and the demons whispering in your ear about the pain you've experienced.

Alcohol has been commonly referred to as "liquid courage" because it gives people permission to do and say things while under the influence of alcohol that they would not otherwise do in a sober state. It also can give people a sense of invincibility. Intoxicants reduce people's inhibitions and impair one's judgment. Because inhibitions are suppressed by intoxicants, people are less able to calculate risk or use good judgment about the words they say or things they do.

There's a running joke that says if you want to know how someone really feels, get them drunk. When you're intoxicated, you feel free to express your thoughts and feelings without the normal mental filters that facilitate good judgment. And when you tell them about what they did when they were intoxicated, they are shocked and maybe even feel embarrassed and ashamed.

One of the problems with the utilization of alcoholic beverages or drugs as coping mechanisms for pain is that once the drugs and alcohol wear off, the problems, pain or lack of confidence is still there. The problems didn't evaporate while you were intoxicated. When you sober up, they will be there waiting for you. For some people, this temporary relief is worth it because they are in so much emotional pain. However, what's deceptive about this strategy is it can become habit forming and a dependence can develop. Before long, you "need" the drugs or alcoholic beverages to function. Before long, it has grown into a full-blown addiction and it's harder to escape the grip of the intoxicant. I know, I know. "But I can quit whenever I want" many argue. With this continued belief, the addiction eventually will have gained more control over you, than you have over it.

Addiction typically does not develop overnight. Substance use usually starts small but then it grows over time to the point that it becomes an addiction. That's why I titled this trap as the "deception" of intoxication. Societal norms and peer pressure normalize the use of drugs and alcohol, making it even more difficult to detect the deception. When people become more and more dependent on the intoxicant to manage their emotions, it makes it even harder to deal with the stressors of life.

When you go out for casual drinks or use drugs for recreational purposes, understand the risk you're taking. Most of the people who are struggling alcoholics or drug addicts would probably tell you they didn't start drinking or start using drugs with the intent of becoming addicted and dependent upon them. They likely did not intend to destroy their lives, their families, their careers, etc., because of their addiction. But as life kept happening, the pain kept coming and the negative experiences in life created an opportunity for the drugs and alcohol to serve a more prominent role in their lives to help them cope. Over time, hopelessness may have slipped in, making their situation look far more dire than it may have been in actuality. Can I give you a word of advice? Never take advice from yourself when you're in a bad place emotionally. It's usually wrong.

Am I suggesting you can't occasionally have a drink? Of course not. I simply want you to be mindful of the trap it sets.

Trap #5: The trap of impatience.

If you're over the age of two, you know how difficult it is to wait for the things you want. From the time we were able to communicate as small children, we've demanded the things we wanted, and gosh darn it they needed to happen immediately as far as we were concerned. A small baby will scream loud enough to stop their parents in their tracks if they are hungry. That baby doesn't care what the parent is doing, it demands immediate attention. Toddlers are notorious for having tantrums and outbursts when they can't get what they want as soon as they have the urge or desire for it. We're born with a tendency towards impatience. As we grow up, we still want immediate results; however, as we mature, we learn how to manage our expectations a bit better. Most of us eventually learn how to tame our temper tantrums, at least most of the time.

Come with me for a second and let's take a stroll down memory lane for a moment if you don't mind. Go back as far as you can and think back on most of the things you got in trouble for. Think about the regrets you have for the things you did. Think about the money you've wasted on things you had to have at the time and now you don't even use it anymore. Think about the relationships you entered into that you knew were not right for you. Think about some of the jobs you took out of desperation only later to hate that you ever worked there. Want to take a guess at what they all have in common? I'll take a stab at it. If you look underneath the surface, and peel a few layers back, you'll likely find an element of impatience. Or perhaps you're more familiar with the phrase "...immediate gratification..." – it was likely an inability to delay something. The decisions to act, buy, say, or do what we did was likely due to our inability to wait patiently for the right time and context to get the things we desired. We rushed to get it, do it, say it, buy it, etc., only to later realize we should have waited.

We are moved by our impulses and a sense of urgency that demands we get the things we want immediately. This is commonly referred to as a "microwave society," which means most people want things instantaneously. Think about it. A meal takes 2-3 minutes in the microwave to cook, but a good home cooked meal can take up to an hour to prepare or longer. Because we don't have the patience or time to wait that long to eat, we settle for something quick in the microwave or unhealthy fast-food. Unfortunately, this behavior and mindset transfers to other areas of our life.

With the utilization of social media today, we have grown accustomed to snippets and sound bites and now that's how many people communicate. Any written communication longer than a few sentences gets overlooked because it takes too long to get to the point. A video, podcast or sermon has to fit within a small window of time before the audience loses interest. Why? Because we have a tendency to turn our attention elsewhere lest we miss something happening somewhere else. We have been unconsciously conditioned by social media outlets to limit our engagement to 30 second videos, two sentences of written text and one-to-two-minute drama filled stories. Anything beyond that will be scrolled over in a search for the next thing to captivate our attention. Yet, the irony in all this is that we will spend countless hours scrolling social media for the next thing, but won't spend 5 minutes on one particular post, article, podcast, book, etc. Hmmm...

As a result of this growing appetite for immediate results, we now have a society that's super impulsive, quick tempered, angry, spoiled, violent and in massive amounts of debt. Young ladies are giving up the most sacred part of their bodies to boys and men outside of a marital context and consequently having children born and raised without the father involved. Why? Because of impatience.

I can hear someone now with a counter-argument against waiting. Before you assault me, just hear me out. I get my inspiration from my own lived experiences combined with what the scriptures teach about patience and I've realized being impatient is very expensive at times. If, however, on your journey back in time through your life, you did not make any mistakes, you never made any impulsive decisions that you later regretted, you were always slow to speak and quick to listen and you always waited for the perfect time to do, act or say, then this particular trap may not be relevant to you. Please forgive me. But for the rest of us, it's a trap that we've all encountered that has been costly both financially and emotionally.

There are plenty of other traps out there, but I wanted to focus on 5 traps that can be easily overlooked to the point that we do not realize their impact on our lives. Schools certainly don't address these issues in any meaningful way to prepare us. I pray as you were reading them, you were able to connect and relate to them in your own way. Of course, no one will have the same experiences, but I tried to be broad enough to touch on everyone at some point. Since we were just talking about impatience, I know you can't wait to get to the next life lesson on relationships. Come on over to this next lesson and see how different relationships play a role in our lives.

LIFE LESSON SIX

Relationships – Our Greatest Assets

Regardless of how much of a maverick you want to be or think you are, we all know we can't survive and thrive without relationships. Remember earlier when I talked about Adam in the creation story and how he was alone? God saw the man being alone with no one to relate to and said "it is not good for man to be alone." The fact is, we need each other. Relationships are essential and we must treat them as such. Relationships are some of our greatest assets. Remember what an asset is from earlier? An asset is something or someone that adds value. In this life lesson, I want to talk about key relationships in life and how to value them for what they contribute to our lives.

As is only fitting, I will begin this lesson by discussing the first relationships we ever have: our relationships with our parents. Before I get started, let me put my disclaimers out now. I know this can be a touchy subject for many people due to the complexities of relationships. Some reading this may have had the benefits of being raised in a two-parent household. Some may have been raised by a single parent like myself. Others were adopted and never knew their biological parents. I am aware of the many different scenarios people may have encountered as I write this book, but please keep in mind, I'm primarily trying to highlight the significance of having healthy relationships with our parents if possible. With that being said, let us go to the other side.

Ideally, our parents are our first friends, protectors, coaches, cheerleaders, providers, nurses and heroes among many more things. Parents sacrifice a lot for the betterment of their children, and oftentimes, the children have no idea what the parents have to sacrifice in order to provide them with a better life and better opportunities.

Children are oftentimes the largest investment parents make in a lifetime. If we could calculate the total cost of raising a child from birth to 18-20, most people would probably faint after seeing the number. Our parents put a lot of money, time, effort, sacrifice and delayed gratification into raising us. The only return on investment (ROI) they expect is a functional adult who makes meaningful contributions to society and lives up to their full potential.

Parents want to feel proud of the children they raised. That desire to see their children become successful may be the driving force that keeps them loving and supporting their children as they transition through life. Lord knows the transitions can be difficult. I'm in a transition now with my teenage son who's trying to discover himself as a young man. As a dad, I find myself having to compete with the many other outside influencers in his life. From the music he likes, to the friends he gravitates to, to his hormones being seemingly out of control and his appetite for girls being insatiable. It's a bit too much and at times I want to quit. But I can't because it's a part of the process and I can't skip over it to get to the good side. Raising my son has given me a greater sense of appreciation for what my parents went through as they raised me. Although my mom raised me primarily on her own, my father provided guidance and parenting from a distance as best as he could. I'm fairly certain my parents may have wanted to quit on me several times during my young and immature years, but I'm so glad they didn't give up on me because of my behavior. Because my parents made it successfully through the parenting stage, I know I can, too.

If you had good parents and you have a meaningful relationship with them, take a moment right now to thank them. Pause your reading and call your parents and thank them for all the sacrifices they made for you. You're never too old to tell your parents thank you. And you can never say thank you enough to them. Trust me, it never gets old. I can almost guarantee it will put a huge smile on their face when they hear your sentiments of appreciation. Even for the parents whose smiles are undetectable, your "Thank you!" will register in their heart. That one call could make their investment in your life seem worth it. I promise. When you have that conversation with them, I would absolutely love to hear how it went. Please share your experience with me by contacting me on social media. Now let's talk about another type of relationship that can be quite rewarding and meaningful: Romantic relationships.

Dating & Fishing – What do they have in common?

Being raised in a small town in Lake Providence, Louisiana, I learned how to fish for dinner as a child. Remember, we were poor, so fishing was a necessity. The town is named after the huge lake that runs right through it and that's where I first learned how to fish. As I grew older, I started to notice some similarities between dating and fishing. Going on dates can be fun, exciting and romantic. The newness of the relationship keeps you curious and full of hope. Fishing can be like that too at times. Finding a new fishing spot can be fun, exciting and yes romantic. You're looking for a place to have a great time and hopefully catch a keeper. You don't know exactly what kind of fish are in the water, but you're optimistic and hoping the one you want is in there. When you find a good fishing spot, you want to stay there forever. You become somewhat reluctant to tell others about your "spot" because you don't want them to find out where you catch your fish and start going there all the time.

I remember the first time I went fishing and caught a fish; I was in love. I wanted to go all the time. All I could think about was catching more fish. Of course, not all fishing trips produced the results I desired. Going fishing was one thing. Catching the fish I wanted was an entirely different thing.

Let's take a closer look at other similarities between fishing and dating. In my late teenage and early young adult years, I had the opportunity to go on several dates with different young ladies. Some of the dates were fun and others were not so fun. Some continued on for weeks and months while others ended the same night they began. This was still in my late teenage years, so my hormones were a bit out of control. A lot of my objectives in dating back then was simply engaging in casual sex. But somewhere along the way in my early twenties, I'd grown tired of the casual sex relationships because the young ladies always ended up wanting more than I was willing to commit to.

I was unwilling to commit because I had experienced hurt from a relationship in high school that I thought would last forever. And since that one didn't work out; I built a wall around my emotions to protect myself. The hurt from that failed relationship operated as an anesthesia to my feelings and consequently I became numb and insensitive to any resemblance of love or strong emotions towards anyone.

One lesson I learned from that era in my life and still believe today was that dating was supposed to be purposeful. As I entered my early twenties, I started to see dating as the way in which two people were able to see if they were a good match for a committed relationship. Therefore, when I dated a young lady, I was really interviewing her as a possible wife. If I determined early on that the young lady was not someone, I would be willing to marry, I would end the relationship before we became too emotionally or sexually involved. I didn't want to be hurt again and I also didn't want to hurt others in the process. Those early dating experiences helped me in a lot of ways because they helped me to identify qualities that I was attracted to and what type of women I was more inclined to pursue.

You attract what you want by the bait you use.

I still do a lot of fishing in my spare time. It's therapeutic for me. Plus, I actually eat the fish I catch, so it serves as a dual-purpose hobby. The kind of fish I intentionally try to catch is called a Crappie, which is a fresh-water perch. To me, it is one of the best tasting fish in the water. I enjoy salmon, catfish, flounder, redfish and others, but Crappie is by far my favorite fish. So, let's just say in this analogy, the Crappie to me is the fish I would marry. Everything else is just... you know... fun to catch!

Because I love to eat Crappie, I've learned a thing or two about how to catch them. I learned *what* they like to eat, what they will *not* eat, and *when* they like to eat. I generally know *where* to find them hanging out. I know at times they can be stubborn and no matter how much I beg, they do not comply with my requests because they don't want to be bothered. I've even seen them look at my bait underwater and not touch it. There have been times when they were not in the mood for the bait I was offering but then all of a sudden become aggressive and I can't get my bait to them fast enough. In case you haven't noticed, Crappie can be somewhat moody at times. See, I told you there were a lot of similarities to fishing and dating. Pay close attention to this next part ladies.

The fish I desire to catch are primarily attracted to two types of bait: either live minnows, which are smaller shiny fish, or plastic lures/jigs that look like small fish that Crappie are normally attracted to. I know if I want to catch a Crappie, I have to use one of those two baits. They will not bite anything else because it isn't in their diet. I can bait my hook with a cricket or a worm and they simply will not touch it. Other fish will, but a Crappie won't. Because I know what type of fish I want to catch and I know what it takes to catch them, I have to prepare accordingly. I try to go fishing at optimum feeding time for Crappie, and I take the bait they like. Why do I go through that much effort and intentionality? Because I know exactly what I want to catch.

Now, occasionally a different type of fish like a bass, garfish or catfish will eat my minnow. When that happens, I generally throw the non-Crappie fish back. Why would I do that? Because that fish was not what I was looking for. True enough, the non-Crappie fish I caught wanted what I had, but I didn't want it. Every fish that's attracted to my bait will not go home with me. Did you catch that? I will say it again. Every fish that's attracted to my bait will not go home with me.

Before I go any further, let's talk about the different types of fish you find in freshwater lakes and ponds. The description of the fish below can provide some insight into the types of individuals who are involved in the dating pond.

Catfish: Catfish are what some people refer to as '***bottom feeders***' because they eat both living and dead things that have fallen to the bottom of the lake. If you want to catch catfish, you can use chicken livers, wieners, earthworms or dead minnows and simply cast the bait in the water and let it sink to the bottom where catfish usually gather looking for food. Once they see your bait, they will take it. They are not picky and will eat almost anything.

Bass: Bass are *opportunists.* If you want to catch bass, they tend to swim near the shore or near trees in shallow water. Bass eat smaller fish, but also small reptiles like frogs and lizards as they navigate their way across the water from land. They wait for their prey to become vulnerable and they strike when the prey is at a weak point, unable to defend itself or escape quickly. When bass see easy prey, they attack.

Garfish: These fish are *sneaky.* They will try to slowly take your bait without causing a scene. They have long mouths with sharp teeth which makes it difficult to hook them. Because of their long mouth, they can easily steal your bait and go undetected. The garfish will try to just nibble away your bait until it's all gone. You have to be on high alert with these types of fish because they are hard to catch in the act. Before you know it, your bait is gone and so is the fish.

I'm sure you're saying or thinking 'That's great Derrick, but what do fish patterns and behaviors have to do with dating?' The simple answer is this: For each of the fish mentioned above, there's a person who has a similar style and personality when it comes to dating. And the type of bait you use, where you cast your bait, and how you present your bait when you leave home can determine what you attract. If you are looking for a certain type of partner, then how you present yourself will either attract them or cause them to look the other way. To the ladies, the more revealing you are, the more of the wrong kind of men you're likely to attract. The less clothing you wear, the more catfish, garfish and bass you will attract. Not to say that non-Crappie fish are bad fish, as different people are looking for different types of fish. But if you're not looking for catfish, garfish and bass, then you might want to consider using the bait that works to catch the fish that you like.

Generally, men who are looking for a wife are not attracted to women who dress provocatively and reveal their physical features leaving little to the imagination. Trust me, men know and can recognize a woman with a nice body without you showing it all to them. Men may admire your body and even desire to have sex with you as a one-time event. But if they are looking for a wife, your attire sends a message to them that may not work in your favor. They appreciate sexy attire and there's a time for that, but the sexy attire usually comes after you're already married. Ladies, if you wonder why you keep attracting the wrong type of men, perhaps, I mean just consider and evaluate the bait you're using and the environments you hang around. Men, if you keep attracting the wrong type of women, perhaps you should consider the places you frequent and the bait you're using. Just consider it.

Catch and release

There are two types of fishermen. The first type are the people who fish purely for the sport of it. We'll call them the 'catchers' for this illustration. They have no desire to keep or eat the fish they catch. They simply enjoy the thrill of the catch. The second type of fishermen are those, who like me, fish because they want to eat the fish. We'll call them the 'consumers.' Consumers actually want to take the prize home. We will wait for hours to catch just one of the right kind of fish. We love the process of preparing to catch the fish, we love catching the fish, and we love eating the fish.

Similarly, there are two types of people in the dating world. The consumers or 'keepers' are those who date in search of compatibility and the potential for a deeper commitment (which is marriage) and the catch and release or 'catchers' are those who enjoy the thrill of the catch. They both have an idea of the kind of person they want to catch and release or catch and commit. Both fishermen know where the fish they want generally hangs out. They both know when is the best time to find them, and both try to offer what attracts the kind of person they want. The primary difference between the 'keeper' and the 'catcher' is the purpose for the date. The catcher goes on a date for entertainment and they have no intentions of anything other than a quick thrill and maybe a picture with what they caught. After they've stuck their hook in you and got what they want, they will release you back into the water where they found you.

The problem with catch and release fishing is this. Every time you hook a fish in its mouth you cause the fish pain. The 'catcher' is excited for the moment, but it may be hard for the fish to eat for a little while because of the injuries they sustained when they were caught. You see, fishing for sport or catch and release results in fish being injured and wounded. They may be traumatized by the experience and become very skeptical of every other bait they see because of the pain they experienced at the hands of the catch and release fisherman. The fish who survive will inevitably bite again because they have to eat. But each time they bite bait and end up getting caught and released again, more damage is done to their mouth and they become more and more traumatized. This pain and trauma can cause the fish to stop biting even when they see the bait they like. Unfortunately for the fishermen who are fishing to consume or commit, the fish that they are looking for won't bite because they've been hurt too many times.

How many times has this happened in dating relationships? How many ladies have been hooked, caught and released by men who went looking for a thrill? Like the fish that were thrown back, the ladies had to go back feeling rejected and unwanted into the environment where they were caught. How many men have waited for the right one and they never showed up because they had already been hurt too many times by the catch and release men? Or they did catch one, but it had so much previous damage from the catch and release guys, they had a hard time accepting them because they could tell someone else has hooked them multiple times before. Can you see it better now?

Attention young ladies, this part is especially for you, so please listen up. In all of my fishing days, I've never seen a Crappie jump out the water, splash around or do anything to let me know they were in the area like some of the other fish will do. They are not trying to get attention by doing things that are unnatural just to get noticed. From my experience, if the fisherman wants to catch a Crappie, they gotta be willing to put in some effort to find them. You have to come correct to even get their attention, and you have to bring something to the table that's appealing. When you are a prize, the ones seeking to gain the prize will pay the price to get what they want.

You my dear are a prize! Don't compromise your value because you're not easily seen jumping around trying to get attention and you don't hang around places where opportunists lurk like the bass. Don't compromise your value and just accept anything tossed in front of you like the catfish. Don't compromise your value and allow boys or young men to "practice" with you and steal your bait like the garfish. Don't let them perfect their cast, stroke and hook setting techniques with you only to send you back to where you came from and then go marry a Crappie when they are ready. Be the CRAPPIE!

Are you starting to see the similarities better now? Can you see how some people have similar characteristics of fish? Can you see how getting into a lot of relationships just for entertainment can cause long term damage to people? What's your taka-away from this?

Let's go a little deeper into romantic relationships and talk about marriage.

Marriage – Is it for me?

The sanctity of marriage has been established for thousands of years and it has served as the foundation for which families are built upon. To fall blissfully in love with your absolute perfect soulmate, have three beautiful children, have a gorgeous home complete with a white picket fence and two nice luxury vehicles in the garage seems like a dream life for some people. Yet others detest the thought of being tied down to one person for the rest of their lives.

In light of evolving cultural shifts, the rising divorce rate and the emergence of gender manipulation, is marriage, as traditionally defined, still a valuable or necessary social structure? Why is there such a contrast concerning marriage when it is such a significant contributor to our societal and cultural norms? Is it right for you? Let's talk about it.

What is marriage?

By technical definition, a marriage is defined as the legally or formally recognized union of two people as partners in a personal relationship (historically and in some jurisdictions specifically a union between a man and a woman). For the sake of this writing, when I refer to marriage, I will be referring to a man and a woman.

I will attempt to address the topic of marriage with the goal of painting a more realistic picture of what marriage is and what marriage isn't so those of you who want to get married can have a better idea of what you're getting into if the opportunity for marriage arises. And for those of you who are already married, hopefully I can help to strengthen your marital relationship with some of the information I provide.

For now, I beg of you to allow me to forgo the romanticized version of marriage. A trillion books have been written that talk about the fantasized version of unwavering love, passion, and limitless romance. I want to get to the meatier matters of marriage; the matters where many of us have been UNDER EDUCATED. So, let's dive in, shall we?

Marriage encompasses many different things that go much deeper than the surface and artificial stuff we see far too often. In order for a marriage to work properly, all of the essential pieces need to be in place and each "piece," or what I refer to as pillars, must be in healthy shape. If you've ever been to the beach, undoubtedly, you've seen homes built on pillars. These pillars, or beams, can be made of concrete, treated wood or both. Concrete pillars are reinforced with steel rebar because of the weight of the house they will carry.

Each home will usually be supported by four of these pillars – each one being responsible for carrying a portion of the weight of that home. During the building process, these pillars are driven deep into the ground until they rest on solid earth. Then they are surrounded with concrete to help stabilize and secure them further. There may be other structural supports underneath the home, but the majority of the weight of the home rests on these four support pillars.

No matter how nice the home is on top, if the pillars underneath the home are unstable, that nice home will eventually collapse and be destroyed. Marriage is like this in a lot of ways. There are **four foundational pillars** that carry the bulk of the weight of the relationship. As we discuss this further, I want you to keep in mind the role of pillars.

Pillar One: Can I trust you?

First, let's talk about trust. Trust is one of the foundational pillars of a strong healthy marriage. If there are trust issues before you get married, do yourself a favor and leave now. Until you resolve your trust issues, you are setting yourself and the marriage up for failure right out the gate. You have to be able to trust your spouse with your very life. You need to feel confident that your spouse will always do what's in your best interest, including protecting your emotions. I'm not saying they will be perfect or they won't make mistakes, but you must have confidence that they will never intentionally do anything to hurt you and they only want what's best for you. If you don't have this level of trust in them or them in you, all of the superficial features that attracted you to them will eventually fade away. You will find yourself miserable and isolated with a bunch of negative thoughts about your spouse, and over time those negative thoughts will invite the rest of the "negative thought family" to the party taking place in your mind: Resentment, lies, pettiness, revenge, malice, and even assault if the negative thoughts go too long untreated.

Small cuts can kill too.

It doesn't take a large laceration to kill someone. Multiple small cuts can cause a person to lose too much blood and lead to a slow death. What does this have to do with trust? Sometimes it's the little things, those small cuts, that break down trust. Small cuts consist of things like asking your spouse to take the trash out and they forget or asking them to wash your favorite jersey so you can wear it later and they forgot. Forgetting to show your spouse needed affection. Publicly embarrassing them or shaming them for entertainment. Forgetting to pay a bill that leads to late fees or a service disconnection or being late to a scheduled event when one spouse knows how important punctuality is to the other spouse can all contribute to small cuts in the relationship. Small cuts may come in the form of perpetual financial mismanagement and lack of awareness leading to wasteful spending or forgetting to assure your spouse that you still desire them and find them physically attractive. I could go on, but I hope you're starting to see what I mean by small cuts. It's the little things that go unnoticed. Some may call them signs. If you're not paying attention, you may miss them or overlook them or simply normalize the behavior to the point you don't realize your spouse is bleeding out from the small cuts.

While many married couples still exist physically, emotionally they look like they've had an altercation with a ninja warrior and lost. They may not have any gaping cuts that would be easily identifiable as the single source that caused the death of the relationship, but those small cuts are there. If you're in a committed relationship for a long period of time, you're going to get cut. That's inevitable. We're human and we often cut the people we love unintentionally. However, too many small cuts can be detrimental to a relationship over time, and only an autopsy will reveal which cut was the final one that killed the relationship.

Pillar Two: Commitment – Are you able to truly Commit?

Commitment is another foundational pillar to marriage. Solid commitment is key if you desire to have a lasting relationship that can stand the test of time and endure the challenges that come with co-inhabiting a space together on a daily basis. You and your spouse need to assure one another that you are committed for the long haul and that nothing will tear down that commitment. If your spouse senses cracks in the foundation because of lack of commitment, it can cause irreparable damages to the relationship. Even the very hint at the marriage breaking up can be catastrophic to the relationship. Your spouse has to know that no matter what, you will not leave them stranded. You have to pre-determine that divorce is not an option and vow to NEVER bring it up as an option. Under any circumstances! NEVER! The moment that you introduce the thought of divorce, your relationship will never be the same.

It takes a lot for someone to become vulnerable to the point that they are willing to forsake all others and commit to one person for the rest of their life. That's not something to be taken for granted. Imagine how low morale would be on a job if every week people were being laid off. People who had been with the company for years were being laid off or threatened to be let go. How much productivity would you get out of them? How committed do you think they would be on the job? Do you think you're going to get their best? It's highly unlikely you'll get anything more than them just showing up and doing the basic requirements to maintain the stability of the income for now. Their heart, however, wouldn't be anywhere near that job. It's similar for marriage. When you introduce divorce and show signs that the marriage is at risk of being terminated, your spouse starts preparing for the termination and their commitment to the marriage diminishes similar to an employee facing termination. This will deteriorate your spouse's trust and lead to additional problems in the relationship.

Pillar Three: Love – What's Love got to with it?

Love is one of the most abused words in our society. We use it recklessly and with utter negligence at times. We "love" everything. Sometimes I think a more accurate depiction of what we are feeling would be "enjoy" instead of "love" because that's most likely the feeling you're experiencing. Try this out really quickly. Say it with me. Are you ready? Say I "enjoy" you. Or maybe "I really ENJOY spending time with you." How did that feel? To me it felt lighter than "love" but still very meaningful. The word enjoy has less of an emotional valence to it, and it is a nice way to say you appreciate something without feeling the pressure to make a premature commitment. I believe use of the word enjoy is more appropriate during the early phases of a developing relationship. Because love is a heavy word, it shouldn't be tossed around so easily.

In dating relationships these days, it's not uncommon to meet someone you're physically attracted to and after one dinner, a walk in the park holding hands, and a kiss on the cheek afterwards, you say you're in love. That's not love my dear. You may have "enjoyed" the experience you had with the person. At best, it may be infatuation (an intense, but short-lived passion or admiration for someone or something). Love, however, runs deep and is not a short fused, temporary feeling of lustful excitement and exhilaration. That type of lust may get you to the altar, but it won't be enough to keep you in a marriage.

Love is an absolute necessity for a healthy marriage. Love in a marriage looks different. Love in a marriage is not the kind of romanticized love you see in Hollywood movies and on social media these days. I believe love in the context of a marriage works best when you practice the biblical kind of love. 1st Corinthians chapter 13, verses 4-8 defines what love is. *"Love is patient, love is kind. It does not envy, it does not boast, it is not proud. It does not dishonor others, it is not self-seeking, it is not easily angered, it keeps no record of wrongs. Love does not delight in evil but rejoices with the truth. It always protects, always trusts, always hopes, always perseveres. Love never fails."* This is what mature love look like. Are you ready to provide this type of love to the person you're dating? If your answer is yes, congratulations. I wish you well in your relationship and much success. If your answer is no, then quit before the relationship gets too messy and becomes more difficult to get out of.

Pillar Four – Communication – Can we talk?

Effective Communication is another foundational pillar needed to build and sustain a great marriage. Unfortunately, most couples have not learned how to communicate effectively, even though they may talk a lot. Communication has many components to it and it is truly a skillset that has to be learned. Just because we talk doesn't mean we naturally know how to communicate with others. It takes time to learn how to speak each other's love language. Many times, we unconsciously develop our style of communication based on our environments and our culture. We have to be mindful of this as we enter into marital relationships.

Here are some examples of *how not* to communicate.

- Out-talking someone doesn't make you a great communicator, as you will likely cause the other party to tap out and be done with the conversation due to your verbosity.
- Having an ability to articulate your thoughts in a clear manner doesn't necessarily make you a good communicator either. Over-articulation of your thoughts could cause the other party to feel inferior to you and they retract and retreat into their shell like a turtle does when it suspects danger.
- Dominating the conversation doesn't make you a great communicator either, as it shows that you lack the ability to reason and hear other perspectives. You may think your ways are perfect and no other contributions are needed, but bullying your way through the conversation does not make you a great communicator. No one likes a bully. Even the meekest people among us can get fed up with a bully and put an end to bullying behavior by leaving the relationship altogether.
- Shutting down and invoking the silent treatment does not make you a great communicator. It shows you're immature and do not have an ability to remain engaged in difficult conversations. Rest assured there will be times when difficult conversations are needed and it's not good practice for you to shut down and go silent.
- Tuning the other person out does not make you a great communicator, as you're acting like a spoiled brat who pouts when they can't have their way. Tuning out communicates to your spouse that what they're sharing with you is not important.
- Yelling and shouting at your spouse does not make you a good communicator. It actually makes you look like an emotional tyrant having a fit.
- Always assuming the victim role is not an effective communication strategy, as it demonstrates a tendency to avoid responsibility for your actions or behavior, choosing instead to use manipulative guilt tactics to solicit empathy.
- Always seeking to "win" the argument or disagreement is a terrible communication strategy. You're talking to your spouse, not a jury in a trial. Though you may win the argument, your spouse may be planning

> their victorious escape out of the relationship. If you win every argument, but lose your spouse, was it worth it?

The truth of the matter is, any one of the behaviors mentioned above can destroy communication with your spouse over time. If we're not intentional, we may default to communication styles inherent in our natural temperaments; however, your default communication style may not match well with your spouse. With that being said, I think it would be a healthy investment for you and your spouse or potential spouse to complete temperament assessments to help you understand one another's communication style better. When you understand how they are wired to communicate, it may help to alleviate a lot of frustration.

My wife is a talker, but I'm not much of a small talk kind of guy. I talk with a purpose. She just talks. I've learned sometimes I have to just listen. I've learned to ask her at times "do you want me to just listen or are you seeking my opinion on this." It has minimized frustration on both sides. If she is just venting and I happen to be the closest person to her, lucky me, I get to hear it. The problem we used to struggle a lot with was, I would listen for the problem so I could offer a solution and be the hero. But that's not what she wanted. She just wanted to talk. And talk. And talk. And talk. And talk. And talk. I had to learn to shut up and listen without offering solutions. Just listen and nod.

Bonus Pillar – Are you compatible?

Compatibility is critical for a relationship to last long-term.

Compatibility is often neglected or perhaps overlooked during the dating phase due to the butterflies and wonderful feelings that come with the early stages of dating. The ability to see a lack of compatibility gets worse when there's sexual intercourse prior to marriage, as sex has a way of putting blinders on and causing us to become temporarily intoxicated. You know people don't make wise decisions when they are intoxicated. After the newness of physical intimacy has come and gone and we have sobered up, what do you have left to hold the relationship together?

Physical compatibility and attraction are important, as you should enjoy who you will be looking at for the rest of your life. However, over time, gravity will interrupt the party and things will change. There may be physical body expansion as the years go by. Wrinkles will creep onto their face. Their appetites and desires may change with age. What was exciting at one age may not carry the same excitement at a different age. Their sexual energy and desire may diminish over time. One day you may wake up and ask who the hell are you and what happened to my spouse? Thinking to yourself; "I married a freak and now I'm sleeping with a mummy."

The more shared goals, desires, passions, hobbies, intellectual and spiritual compatibility you have with your spouse or potential spouse, the greater the odds of you being able to sustain a happy, healthy and fulfilling marriage. Engaging in stimulating conversations with your spouse is a special feeling. Being able to talk about a wide range of topics with them is sexy. Being able to brainstorm ideas and strategies for personal growth can be a turn on. Having discussions about spirituality that don't turn into an argument can be quite romantic. Planning and discussing future goals together instead of complaining about your current situation can be attractive. If you have this level of compatibility with your spouse or potential spouse, congratulations. You have something special. If you don't, it's something that can be worked on. It's not too late to develop compatibility in different areas, but awareness is key. Building compatibility is possible but it may require some difficult conversations and intentionality.

I believe if people had more real and honest conversations about marriage and the requirements to maintain a great marriage, people would either opt out until they are ready, or commit to making it work regardless of the other issues that will arise. And trust me, there will be many other issues that arise. However, if you have the pillars discussed above in place and they are solid and established on a solid foundation, you stand a much better chance of being able to survive the other issues. Of course, it's no guarantee. But you increase the odds tremendously.

When should I get married?

I have two children. A 16-year-old son and a 12-year-old daughter. I've already told them that I don't think they should marry until they are close to 30 years old. Any time prior to that is risky... although not impossible. In actual reality,

I'm not totally committed to a specific age, but I do believe many of the things I discussed earlier should be established with each individual before linking up with someone else in a relationship. If you have your finances in order, your credit is in good standing, you're not bringing a cargo ship full of debt to the marriage, you have your own independent savings and financial goals in place and you share common interest, then you might be ok to marry at a younger age. This, of course, largely depends on each person's maturity level. Keep in mind that people are evolving and you have to be willing to evolve with them. If you marry too soon and the person has not evolved mentally, intellectually, financially, spiritually, and emotionally with you in the relationship, you may face some incompatibility challenges later on in the relationship.

Historically, marriages that start early often end in divorce, primarily because of the aforementioned pillars and the lack of compatibility. But, Derrick, you're wrong! I read that infidelity is the leading cause of divorce and after that it's fights over finances as the number two leading cause of divorce. Where do you come from talking about it's because of the pillars you talked about?

I can see your concern and here's my rebuttal. May I suggest that the violation of one or all of the aforementioned pillars played a major role in one party committing adultery. I would double down and be willing to bet that the fights over finances was a direct result of one of the pillars I mentioned. Infidelity a lot of times is a symptom of a deeper issue in the marriage. There are times that infidelity has nothing to do with the other spouse at all, rather it's an internal desire or motivation that causes one party to step outside the marriage to fulfill a sexual desire or live out a fantasy. Unmet emotional needs can lead to an affair from what they perceived as a void in the relationship and an opportunist showed up at the wrong time to fill that void. Money fights are also a symptom of a much deeper issue in a marriage. I'd be willing to bet there are some underlying trust issues that one spouse has against the other. Infidelity may be what gets the publicity, but the violation likely occurred mentally when one or more of those pillars were assaulted, which often occurs well before the infidelity or the mismanagement of resources that caused money fights. Because we have been UNDER EDUCATED, we overlook the deeper issues and only address what we can see on the surface.

If any one of the pillars above (Trust, Commitment, Communication, Love,

Compatibility) sustains damage or is shattered by blunt force from one party or if one of the pillars simply deteriorates over time due to negligence, it can cause weakness and instability in the relationship. With no intervention, it's just a matter of time before the entire structure will be at risk for collapsing. Everything that has been built on top of the damaged pillars will be destroyed. If you are married now, do some maintenance on your pillars. Pay attention to them and see if there are signs of cracking, deterioration, etc. Do what you have to do to repair the weak areas. Hire an outside inspector (counselor) to examine the relationship to identify areas that need to be strengthened. It's much easier and cheaper to repair a pillar than to rebuild a collapsed structure.

Friends – Learn how to distinguish Friends from Associates

We don't get to choose our parents, siblings, or extended family members. However, we are in total control over who we choose as our friends. For the record, when I say "friend," I'm not talking about the five thousand "friends" you have on Facebook, Tic Tok, Twitter, Instagram, or Snapchat. I'm not talking about your virtual friends. I'm talking about the people who come to your house for Thanksgiving dinner, visit you in the hospital, and come to support you at a loved one's funeral. The friends who will tell you when you're wrong and not care if you are offended with them. The friends who push you past your comfort zone in order to help you achieve your goals.

Do you have anyone that fits these criteria? If you do, take a moment and send them a quick text thanking them for being your friend. Real friends are becoming an increasingly rare breed so I encourage you to let them know you value them. Seriously, send them a text, email, DM, something right now. Notice I didn't say call them. I want you to finish reading the book so a call may get you distracted. I just had a selfish moment. But a quick text message is sufficient.

There's a difference between friends and those with whom you associate. Associates are only slightly higher than your virtual friends. However, they do tend to play a more meaningful role in our lives during particular seasons of life. Associates are cool for social gatherings, parties and activities. I've been blessed to meet a lot of people in my life and I'm fortunate to still have access to several of them. For example, I still have associates who were my best friends in school or in the Navy. As our lives went different directions, however, the dynamics of our friendships changed. And yet they still have value.

Associates are generally people you meet with whom you have something in common. For example, an associate could be someone you went to school with, worked with, served with in the military, attended the same church, etc. You will inevitably meet people who may become your associates because of your interactions in the same environments or contexts. Sometimes, in those contexts we meet people who will eventually become some of our best friends. Associate relationships can start due to common interests, but associates don't automatically convert into friends simply because you have things in common.

Here's how to tell the difference between a friend and an associate.

- A friend will hurt when you hurt. They will literally carry the pain with you emotionally when you are hurting. An associate may learn of your hurt and perhaps tell others about it in a false empathetic way, trying to show they care.
- A friend will support you with their time, resources and skill sets, in order for you to succeed. An associate may observe you, clap with their hands, but will not clap with or invest with their resources to help you.
- A friend will rejoice when you get a promotion or an opportunity to achieve something you've been dreaming about. An associate may secretly hate on you and be envious of your success all while wearing an artificial smile on their face.
- A friend will put some of their skin in the game if they can to help you achieve your goals. An associate may watch you pushing and hope you get there, but will remain a bystander on the sidelines watching you struggle to achieve your goals. But once you make it, they will swear they were there the entire time supporting you.
- A friend will tell you when you are wrong. They love you enough to share an unpopular opinion with you that risks hurting your feelings. An associate may affirm your wrongness because they don't want to be perceived as negative.
- A friend will not let you abort a difficult process and they will hold you

accountable. An associate may join in on your pity party and affirm your desire to give up.

- A friend won't allow you to do something stupid that will be detrimental to your well-being. An associate may see you're about to do something stupid and pull out their phone to record it for social media likes.
- A friend won't encourage you to do something that will get you in trouble. An associate may encourage you to do it because they're afraid to do it.
- A friend will try to encourage you to do right in your relationship. An associate may help you justify your misdeeds because they are living vicariously through you.

Being able to discern the differences between friends and associates will help you navigate your paths better in life. Associates have a role to play, but you need to know their role and not allow them to get outside of their role. Appreciate both, but know who to keep close in your inner circle. Set some boundaries for your associates.

You are who you hang around.

It has been said, if you show me your five closest friends, I can predict your future. How is that possible? We as human beings gravitate to like-minded people. Whatever the dominant thoughts, behaviors and values are in your circles, that's likely how you will behave. Because humans are social beings, we generally want to feel accepted by our community. As such, we adjust to fit in.

There's usually something you see in the community of friends that resonates with you.

If you break down the word community, you'll see that it is a combination of two words. Common and Unity. The community you spend the majority of your time with will have something in common that unites everyone in the community. Most likely, your community of friends has many things in common. It could be music, sports, style, struggle, gang affiliation, religion, political views, work or a similar belief system.

Belonging to a community that inspires positive and productive behaviors is wonderful. However, if you are a part of a community whose values cause you to make poor decisions and influence you against everything you know to be right, then that community is not a good community for you and you should avoid bringing bad influences into your circle. When determining who your real friends are, you have to be intentional about selecting who will become a part of your community of friends. If the people in your circle don't fit the criteria I discussed, then it might be a good time to cut ties and build a new friendship circle. It may be painful to cut off some toxic friends, but I assure you this temporary pain will not last nearly as long as the pain of keeping them around you so they can potentially ruin your life and cause you to miss out on great opportunities because of your affiliation with them.

Are you able to distinguish the difference between your friends and associates now? Can you see how dating impacts your life and the life of others? Do you value the investment your parents made in your life? Are you able to appreciate the value of significant relationships in your life? I hope as you were reading this life lesson, you were able to identify the people in your life who mean you well and those who are an asset to you. Keep them close and always appreciate them.

We are near the end of the book with only one lesson left. It's going to be great. Let's finish strong. Come on over to the next lesson. These are essential skills needed to navigate successfully through life.

LIFE LESSON SEVEN

Life Skills Needed to Survive and Thrive

Skill ONE: Conflict Resolution – To fight or not to fight

Whenever there are two or more people in a space, conflict is inevitable. Why? Because we're human and we all have unique life experiences that shape and influence our desires, expectations, wants, likes, etc. that may be different and may conflict with other people's experiences.

If you will allow me to use my spiritual imagination briefly, I'd like to give you something to ponder for a moment just to show how much conflict is part of the human experience. If you're familiar with the story of creation, you'll recall that God instructed Adam to not eat from the tree of knowledge of good and evil, and then Adam told Eve (his wife) what God said about not eating from the tree. At some point, the devil disguised as a serpent made a cameo appearance and introduced an alternative perspective to Eve, which made her question what Adam told her about the tree. Exposure to a different alternative created a conflict within Eve, and she began to wrestle with what Adam said God said versus what the serpent said that appealed to her desires. As fate would have it, Eve's desire to gain the knowledge that the serpent promised got the best of her and Eve ate the forbidden fruit. If I was in church, I'd say "look to your neighbor and say conflict."

After eating the forbidden fruit, Eve suffered no immediate consequence. Somewhat proving the serpent's point, right? She had been enlightened and she was still alive. She, in her excitement about this new insight, wanted to share this experience with her husband Adam. Now, I imagine Adam was experiencing some internal conflict of his own at this point. He's looking at Eve chewing fruit from the tree that God told him would cause death, yet she's standing there naked, her eyes glistening, and with juice running down her lips enjoying the sweet nectar from this forbidden fruit. With all of this temptation, Adam gave in and ate. Immediately, he felt a separation from God and guilt set in as he realized he had violated God's command.

Thus, he went and hid himself and covered himself with leaves, suddenly feeling ashamed. I'm willing to bet Adam and Eve had a heated argument while they were hiding and the consequence of their disobedience began to set in. How do I know this? When God began to question Adam about his whereabouts, Adam instantly blamed God for "That woman YOU gave me." In essence, Adam was saying, "God, you gave me this dang woman and now look at me. This is your fault!" Eve followed suit and shifted the blame to the serpent. They are the only two human beings on the planet and already there's major conflict.

I shared this narrative with you to show you how inherent conflict is within human relationships – even when there are only two people in existence. Since the beginning of time, humans have had conflicts with each other. That part is inevitable. How you deal with and manage the relationship in the context of conflict is more important. So, the goal is not to avoid conflict with others but to learn how to maintain the relationship after the conflict.

How to practically resolve conflict:

As mentioned earlier, avoiding conflict is not the goal. The key to conflict management is being open to consider other points of view. In the midst of conflict, your vantage point is determined by where you are standing. Consider the number 9. On one side it's a nine (9), but someone standing on the complete opposite side sees a six (6). Which one is right? Both. It all depends on the angle you're looking from. My point is this – be open to at least consider the other person's vantage point.

Remember, you don't have to win every debate or prove your point all the time. One way I resolve conflict is to examine the conflict so I can really understand what is this about? After I determine what the root cause of the conflict is, I make another assessment about the potential impact of the conflict?

Depending on what the core issue is and the impact this conflict will have, I then determine if a continued argument, discussion, or conversation is even necessary.

A less convoluted way I do this is by simply asking myself "Why are we talking about this?" By asking myself this question I am able to detach emotionally from certain conflicts that arise and not take them so personal.

Generally, our most intense conflicts will occur with people we are in close proximity to, be it at home, school, work, church, or within our social circles. The reason we get into conflict with these individuals is because, at some level, we care about them. If you are quick to get into intensive conflicts with a complete stranger, you might have anger issues. Seriously, if you find yourself frequently cursing out strangers and wanting to harm them, you need to see a counselor, pastor, friend or somebody.

When it comes to people we are in close relationship with, sometimes you have to be willing to let them maintain their position on the matter, especially if it's not something that negatively impacts your life in a harmful way. Many times, people fall out with each other over matters that, at the core, have no impact on their personal lives – like religion or politics. These two topics are taboo and forbidden as topics of discussion by many people because of the strong opinions and views held by those discussing them. However, at the core of the matter, who you vote for, or why you believe your political party is better than another party has absolutely no impact on my personal life or household economy. The same applies to religion. If you don't believe in God, or if you believe in a different god, that has absolutely no impact on my life or belief in God. You are entitled to your opinion and I'm entitled to mine. As long as you don't try to superimpose your beliefs on me and I don't force mine on you, why are we arguing again? We have to cut out all this hostility over meaningless differences of opinion or beliefs.

Marriages, families and entire countries have been destroyed over insignificant conflicts that were, at the core, simply a difference in beliefs. We don't always have to be right! Just for a moment consider what might happen if you were to acknowledge that the other person's point of view is valid from their perspective. This small step will likely remove some of the hostile energy surrounding the topic.

It can be helpful to give people room to grow and mature as they navigate the challenges of life. If you're right and they are dead wrong, let life teach them without you getting into knock-down, drag-out fights. Leave room for them to come back and acknowledge their wrong if they choose to do so. But if you beat them down to prove they're wrong, even if they realize later that they were wrong, you likely have sealed the door shut and they may not choose to come back to restore the relationship. Let them have their opinion and move on. I know I've held some very strong positions about things in life that I swore I would never do. And I believed I was right until I found myself doing the very thing, I said I would NEVER do. As I've grown wiser over the years, I try to extend to others the same grace I once needed for my wrong perspectives. And you know what I've found? Doing so helps minimize conflicts, and prevents losing relationships. We need each other. Relationships are our most valuable resource.

Skill TWO: Asking the RIGHT QUESTIONS

Questions are one of the tools used to solve some of life's most complex problems. Questions lead to discovering the mystery behind unknown things. Questions are designed to trigger our minds to search for a solution to a problem. Questions are frequently asked by people who are identified as critical thinkers. Asking the right question can produce the right answer when you're dealing with a complex or confusing situation.

For example, you can ask the question "Why did you do that?" in different ways. You may ask the question in search of a justification from the person. That same question could be asked in an investigative manner trying to discover a motive. One is accusatory and the other is exploratory. One will produce an excuse and the other will produce an understanding. Depending on how you ask the question, you may get different responses.

Based on this fact, when I speak of asking yourself the right questions, I am referring to the questions that will lead you to explore why and then lead to a solution. Here's an example. If you ask yourself "Why haven't I reached my financial goals for the year?" your mind might initially produce an excuse and look to blame someone or some external circumstance to justify why you haven't reached your goal. If your mind is conditioned to ask the right question, your response might be, "...because I didn't write my goals down, I didn't use a budget, I didn't delay gratification and I spent more money than I prioritized saving..." If you are honest with yourself and don't allow your mind to manipulate you, the right question will produce the right answers.

Here's an example of a better way to ask a question that could help me reach my financial goal. "What are some things I can do starting now to achieve my goals?" Asking the question in this way will likely trigger your mind to start looking for solutions rather than excuses?

Here's another example. Why am I overweight? The excuse will sound like "...because I'm big boned..." or "...its genetics...." The other answer could be "because I eat too many processed foods loaded with carbs, sugars, fats, etc. I don't have a regular exercise regimen." A better question might be, "What are small things I can do to start cutting out unhealthy eating so I can lose weight?" "Where can I schedule 30 minutes in my day to exercise?" Do you see what happened with reframing the question? The questions are shifting your mind towards reasonable solutions to the problems.

One more example. Why do I keep losing my job or getting overlooked for the promotion? The excuse response will sound something like "...it's because they don't like me..." or "...they're hating on me..." A reframed question would sound like "What more can I do, or what other value can I add to the company or organization where my contributions would justify a raise or promotion?" Asking the right question takes the blame off of others and places the responsibility to fix things squarely on you. It moves you from a victim mentality and creates opportunities for you to take full responsibility for the outcomes you seek. Here are a few questions you can ask yourself in almost any situation that may be helpful in moving you in your desired direction.

How can I?

I've taught my children to ask this question since they were old enough to form sentences and ask for stuff. In my house, if you are old enough to ask for stuff, you're old enough to work. My son is the oldest, so he got the first batch. He would ask me "Daddy can you buy me..." and my response was son you're asking the wrong question. Of course, I can buy it. But that's not how life works. You can't just ask life to give you something without first investing something in exchange for what you want. I taught him to ask me the right question and he was more likely to get what he desired. I taught him to ask "How can I earn some money to buy ..." Now you're speaking my language, son. When he asked me to help him identify an opportunity for him to work for something he wanted, I happily found a way for him to earn money so he could buy the things he wanted. His desire to earn money to buy the things he wanted caused me to fire my lawn guy and help my son start a lawn business.

I intentionally taught my children how to "ask for opportunities" to earn money to purchase what they wanted because I didn't want to handicap my children into thinking life was simply going to give them something for nothing. That's not how it goes. Agriculture teaches us this principle. You plant an apple seed in soil, and the soil will give you a fruit tree. If you don't plant the seed, the soil has no obligation to produce fruit for you. So, when you ask the question "How can I?" you are saying what must I do or contribute to position myself to achieve my desired outcome.

Why not me?

For many years I suffered from low self-confidence. I don't exactly know when it originated or what the source of it was. I just know I dealt with it. When I was younger, I didn't have a label to put on what I was feeling. I just knew I was experiencing the results of this feeling. Because of my low self-confidence, I often would talk myself out of things that I really wanted because I was afraid of failure and rejection. Including asking my high school crush for her phone number.

Somewhere along my life's journey, I began asking the question: Why not me? After some soul searching and uncomfortable dialogue with myself, I concluded that I did not achieve some of the things I wanted to because I chose not to attempt them. ***I never even tried! I was my own biggest enemy***. My fear of rejection had me playing it safe and small. I would allow fear and doubt to dominate my thoughts and cause me to remain paralyzed.

When we are able to confront our debilitating thoughts and overcome our inner doubt, we realize the only thing holding us back is us. The things you want to accomplish may seem scary, but it's only scary because you haven't done it yet. You can accomplish far more than you believe you can by asking yourself the question Why not me?

I guarantee once you do it, you will look back at the once daunting obstacle and smile. Truth be told, that was my experience when I wrote my first book *Unlock Your Mind, Unlock Your Money*. I had never written a paper longer than ten pages for a school project before, so how was I going to write a book? But remember when I mentioned earlier in the relationship section about how you become like the people you hang around? I was in an environment of people I knew who had written books, so that exposure helped boost my confidence, and consequently I produced a best-selling book. After I finished the book and held it in my hands for the first time, I felt invincible. All of the doubts and insecurities were gone. I felt this great sense of accomplishment and I was one proud man.

What can I do?

This is another powerful question to ask yourself. "What can I do?" forces you to identify ways to accomplish a goal. Instead of manifesting a self-fulfilling prophecy of defeat, ask yourself the question: What Can I do? Take a moment and think about something you want to accomplish or a goal you want to achieve and then ask yourself, what can I do to achieve it? NOW PAUSE AND ANSWER THE QUESTION.

Did your brain immediately start searching for options? Even though the answers may not have come immediately, the fact that you gave your brain permission to search for solutions creates an opportunity to achieve more and accomplish more than you may have previously imagined. Trust me your brain is constantly processing and searching for ways to achieve what you told it you wanted even when you're not consciously thinking about it.

I remember back in the summer of 2008 right around the time when the housing market crashed. I was a full-time real estate agent, which meant my income was based solely on commissions and not a stable salary. I worked primarily with investors and during the market crash, my clients couldn't get loans to purchase properties because the banks were nervous about loaning money to investors due to the nationwide foreclosures on homes. At the time, I had a 3-year-old child and I had gone through a foreclosure myself, so my credit was trashed. I couldn't sit around and complain about how hard it was. What good would that do? I had to ask myself "What can I do to earn a living for my family?" After examining all the options on the table, I pursued the best option, which was becoming a police officer. One year later I was going to bootcamp at the Houston Police Department where I served as a patrol officer for 5.5 years before getting injured and being forced to medically retire.

That one question of "What can I do?" to earn money for my family has literally put over one-million dollars in my pocket since then. In that season of the housing market crashing, which essentially made me unemployed, if I hadn't asked myself the right questions, I could have easily labeled myself as a failure and started my own pity party. But I didn't. I had to pivot and find new ways to generate income for my family, so failure was not an option. And speaking of failure, let's talk about that too.

Skill THREE: Embracing Failure

When it comes to failure, it can truly be a paralyzing fear. But what exactly is failure? Failure is a mental construct that suggests we did not achieve success or the results we were in pursuit of. How we generally define failure is results driven and it does not take into account progress. Oftentimes, progress is not measured or given any credit when people think about failure. In school, we were given tests that are designed to examine our comprehension of a particular subject matter. Based on how well we answered the questions during the examination, we either passed or failed. Being conditioned to see life as pass or fail can produce mental obstacles or limitations at an early developmental stage. This system of pass or fail is embedded in us early on in grade school. The problem with this perspective is that it does not convert as easily in the real world. There's more than one way to come up with a correct answer.

As a result of this conditioning of pass or fail, in the real world, we may feel inadequately prepared for success. And because we are afraid of failing, we play it safe. We stay in our comfort zones. We only follow the paths that have already been cleared for us. And because of this, many of us are UNDER EDUCATED on how to interpret perceived failure.

Quick question: How many software programs did Bill Gates and his team come up with before they figured out Microsoft? How many cars did Elon Musk create and destroy while trying to perfect a totally electric car? How many shots did Michael Jordan miss before becoming one of the most recognizable names in sports history? Did these people fail? Yes, based on how we traditionally define failure. But they understood the risk of being perceived as a failure was built into the process of achieving greatness. They chose to not cower under the threat of failure and embarrassment. They chose to not allow their fears, doubts and unbelief to drown out their confidence. They DID NOT QUIT!

Failure is a mental bully!

The threat of failure sits around and dares you to try something different or new. It has a way of making things scarier than they really are, like the school yard bully who walks around and uses their size to intimidate smaller kids. I remember getting into a fight with a school bully. I tried to avoid him most days, but there was one day in particular when he started his antics in the cafeteria early in the day. By the end of the school day, I determined that I had been living in fear long enough. I was no longer going to walk around school in fear. During the last period of school, I walked into class and, there he was mocking me for some unknown reason. After several verbal insults meant to embarrass me and solicit laughs from others, he escalated the situation and walked over to me and pushed me. Without consulting with any of the faculties in my body, I instinctively fought back. I remember grabbing him by his throat with both hands and pushing him backwards across several desks. I remember straddling him on the floor and I was trying to choke the life out of him in my rage. I had determined that I was going to put an end to this school terrorist. The teacher eventually broke it up, but not before I was able to establish that I wasn't afraid anymore and I also got in a few extra punches. In the moment, filled with rage and adrenaline, I had no fear. I was fed up! After the final bell rang, school was over, and there he was, along with a growing crowd of spectators. It's about to go down, I thought. At this point, I had already determined I was going to have to confront this dude and that we needed to finish the fight he started earlier. As I approached the crowd, I saw him standing there just outside the door all charged up and seeking revenge. Without thinking, my confidence was slightly higher, boom! I punched him in the face. He punched me back in the face, and then we wrestled for a minute until someone broke it up. From that day on, we became good friends. Had I not been provoked to confront the bully; I would have continued living in fear at school. But I decided that I was no longer willing to live in fear. He had intimidated me to the point that I found the courage to face my fears. I had nothing to lose at that point.

It's intimidating to our pride and ego to be perceived as a failure or failing. The very thought of failing has killed more dreams than anything else in history. So many great ideas are in the cemetery because they died with the originator. Why did the idea die? They were afraid of trying and potentially failing. They procrastinated too long because they were afraid of failing. They never confronted their bully. What's mentally bullying you? Will you finally confront it? (I'm not endorsing violence towards a literal person/bully)

I bet you won't

I remember a time in middle school when boys would be intimidated to talk to the pretty girls in school. We would dare our friends to go talk to her. We would even wager a pack of "now and later" candy or a bag of skittles if he successfully engaged her. The pressure to succeed was intense. If the girl publicly rejected you, your chances of hooking up with a different girl was over for the rest of the school year. No other girls would want to talk to him. All of the boys who persuaded him to talk to the girl will sit back and laugh at him for trying. But notice, they themselves were too afraid to try. Yet they were the main ones mocking the boy who at least had the courage to try!

That's how it goes in the adult world too. The characters are different, but the playbook is the same. If you decide to start a business, change how you manage your finances, downsize your lifestyle in order to obtain a bigger vision for your life, those on the sidelines may laugh at you and even mock you for having the audacity to do something outside of the status quo. Unfortunately, many adults are still walking around wounded from childhood rejection they interpreted as a failure. They may have grown in age, but mentally they are still struggling with grade school rejections and failures.

"You will never make it"

When I became a police officer, I had very clear goals of what I was there for. To make a lot of money. Remember, I couldn't depend on my credit anymore because it was ruined by the foreclosure and getting behind on other payments. I had to buy everything with cash. I was fascinated by the potential income I could earn working side jobs or "extra jobs" as they are commonly referred to. I remember graduating from the police academy and I couldn't wait to work an extra job. Unknown to me at the time, I had to wait until I finished one year of probation before I could work an extra job. After my probation year was up, I was off to the races. I worked every side job I could squeeze in on a day-to-day basis. For the first year, I made a lot of money, but I was always away from my family and my sleep was non-existent. This was profitable, but not sustainable. I began to ask questions like "how can I earn the same money, while cutting my time in half?" My uncles were also police officers so they told me about doing police escorts on motorcycles and how much money they made escorting funerals and large trucks on the freeway. That sounded good to me, but there was only one real problem. I didn't know how to ride a motorcycle. Actually, I was somewhat intimidated at the thought of riding a motorcycle. I couldn't comprehend the shifting and remaining stable on two wheels. The thought of it was terrifying.

I talked to a few of my colleagues about me potentially doing escorts, and I was swiftly informed of how hard the course was. Only a handful of people were allowed to ride with the city. Quite frequently I was told things like "They have a clique over there." or "They have a "good ole boy" system over there.", and on and on and on. Needless to say, I was discouraged to pursue it because of the difficulties associated with it, not to mention how many people failed the course before me. I was told "You will never make it." But I thought, what's the worst that can happen? They make three times more money in half the time than my previous extra jobs. That sounded like good math to me, so I inquired about how to get started. I was informed that I had to purchase my own motorcycle and spend my own money to get it equipped with police lights, sirens, etc. Oh yeah, and by the way, there's a motorcycle course you must complete before you can do escorts as a police officer. And on top of that, the course was only offered twice a year.

I thought, "No biggie!" I went out and purchased a used police motorcycle already equipped with lights. I then went to take a basic motorcycle riding course in order to learn how to ride the thing. At this point, I'd already invested nearly $10,000.00 into my new venture so failure was not an option. When I got to the police motor course, after lots of time and money spent in preparation for this semi-annual event, I was ready. As soon as I got to the training grounds, I was informed upon arrival that the motorcycle I had was not qualified because they were just starting to standardize the motorcycles and everyone in the department had to ride a Harley Davidson. Well, I'll be darned. I had a Honda ST 1300. But now, in order to qualify, I would have to buy another motorcycle before I could officially begin to do escorts. However, they allowed me to take the course on the bike I had.

This course was hard! I saw other riders doing things on a motorcycle that I didn't think were possible. Needless to say, I was intimidated – yet again. But I kept reminding myself: "If others can pass this course, so can you." I did well the first few days. After many falls, motorcycle drops or "laying it down" as it's commonly called, I learned many of the maneuvers and my confidence began to increase. I knew the graded riding test came at the end of the week and I had a lot riding on that moment. After a long week of practicing, it was finally test day. The instructors were fair but unforgiving. They showed no mercy. If you failed one portion of the riding course, it was enough to fail the entire exercise. This explained the high failure rate.

The first few courses, I did great. I was doing fine until the last and most difficult course. The dreaded figure 8 course. After the total points were tallied from all of the courses, riders had to have a passing score of 90 points out of 100 to become certified to ride. As fate would have it, my score was 89. 89! I missed it by one point! I failed!

I was deflated, embarrassed and humiliated by failure. The thought of facing those who advised me to not pursue the course in the first place weighed me down. As you can imagine, I heard it all. "I told you so!" and "You thought I was lying?" and yada yada yada. There I was with a motorcycle I couldn't ride for the purpose for which I purchased it. I didn't enjoy riding motorcycles for entertainment. I had only bought my bike to make money. What should I do now? Might as well give up right? Go ahead and add my name to the list of failures, right? Absolutely not! I waited for the next course six months later and I signed up again. This time, I had a whole six months to practice and prepare. The second time I tested, I passed with very high scores.

The determination to succeed cost me a lot financially and emotionally, but I could not afford to allow failure to define me. I did not allow the negativity of my colleagues to deter me from trying again. I had to get over the fact that I had to make payments on a useless motorcycle for six months. I had to tell all my friends and family that I didn't pass the course and listen to their criticism, advice, or whatever they called it. But in spite of all this, I couldn't let failure be the end of my story. I went on to earn over $250,000.00 additional income in a three-year span from that one decision to overcome my fear of riding, overcome my temporary experience of failure and overcome the embarrassment of having to tell my very opinionated colleagues I failed. It was one of the best decisions I've made in my life. I learned so much about resilience, the experience of failure, and the ability to continue on your journey even when others have aborted the course.

If you want to achieve anything beyond what's expected or considered normal, you have to be willing to embrace the fact that failure or being perceived as a failure is built into the process of progress. No one who has achieved any level of greatness in life got to where they are without failure. I'm reminded of how Tyler Perry sold stage plays out of the trunk of his car and wore a costume of an old lady. He produced low budget movies that many deemed as failures, and I'm sure there were people laughing at him. Who's laughing now? He owns an entire movie studio and produces his own movies and plays, and has created opportunities for thousands of people. Oh yeah, let's not forget he's now a BILLIONAIRE!

Final Thoughts:

Well, my friends, we are nearing the end of the book. You've made it through the last lesson. We have safely landed at our destination and I'm grateful for the opportunity to travel with you. We've covered a lot of topics on this journey and I hope the lessons added value to your life in very meaningful and practical ways.

If you're up for it, though, I do have one more connecting thought I'd like to share. Come on over to the next chapter where I address the importance of spirituality and a relationship with God. I promise it will be worth it. Will you join me?

If you choose not to join me in the next chapter and this is your exit, I sincerely want to thank you for coming along this journey with me as I shared 7 life lessons schools forgot to teach us. I pray that any turbulence you may have experienced was only temporary and overall, the slight turbulence was worth it to get to this destination. Thank you again for taking this journey with me.

I pray you were inspired, informed, educated and empowered with knowledge that will make your life easier to navigate. I wish you nothing but the best in life and I encourage you to share this book with your friends and family. Share it with your children. Share it with your parents. Start a book club to discuss it with your friends, church or co-workers. I'm certain it will create some great and meaningful dialogue as you share what you learned, or similar experiences you've had. Listening to others share what helped them from the book can add even greater value to your experience of reading the book. Get all your monies worth from this book by engaging with others.

My goal is to help one million families with this book. Will you partner with me in spreading the word about the benefits of learning these 7 life lessons? I want to help many people avoid the mistakes I made because I was Under Educated. Help me Help others.

For the rest of you who would like to come on over to the bonus lesson, let's go.

BONUS LESSON

The Spiritual Side of Life: Questions We Can't Ask Out Loud

Is there a God?

I personally believe there is a God. I was raised in a Christian household, so God was not a foreign concept to me as a child. As I got older and began to ask questions for myself, I was convinced beyond a reasonable doubt that there must be some greater power or being in existence outside of the human race. Great debates have taken place for centuries trying to understand and articulate what the higher power is. Thus, many people have different names for it. But simple earthly observations will reveal there is some form of intelligent design to life and our existence.

Many people believe different things about how creation came to be. Some believe things just evolved into what we see today. For me personally, I find great difficulty believing things just magically appeared out of nothingness and then magically started to function in an organized, structured way that has lasted for thousands of years without any new interventions. From the solar system, the ecosystem, to the intricate design of the human body, we should all be able to intellectually conclude something outside of human capabilities created this world. You don't have to be a scientist to come to this conclusion. You have to become a scientist and devote years of your life studying and researching in an attempt to disprove intelligent design and the existence of God. Now that takes effort and great intentionality.

It is believed that we start to ask more probing and complicated questions about life, ourselves and creation during our early teenage years. We begin to ask identifying questions like "Who am I?" and "Why am I here?" to name a few. This is normal and healthy. We are searching for meaning in life. We are looking for identity. We are on a quest to discover our purpose and reason for existing. We're searching for the question I ask often, "What's the point to all of this?" This is a crucial stage of development for young teenagers because the conclusions they come to in this phase will help to steer their path and influence their decisions about life as they enter into adulthood. But in all reality, we never really stop asking that question. A handful of people actually discover their God intended purpose and live in it. Others are on a lifelong search trying to discover their purpose. I believe God has a plan and a purpose for each of us, and it is our responsibility to seek God for guidance and directions to get us to that purpose.

Where can I find out more about God?

Since this is my book, I will steer you to the source that has enabled me to get a better understanding about God. I would recommend and encourage you to seek a church in your area if possible that has a strong emphasis on teaching the bible to you for understanding. Most churches are open to the public and you don't need a reservation to enter. They should welcome you with a warm smile and open arms. If you are unable to find a church, the advancement of technology provides options to attend church services online. God is not hard to find if you are diligently looking for Him.

Are there benefits to reading the bible?

Of course, there are benefits. Some have described the bible as God's love letter to man, that is filled with wisdom and guidance for living an abundant life. It teaches us how to relate to God. It teaches us how to relate to each other. It teaches us how to relate to money. It teaches us how to deal with trials and tribulations. It teaches us how to love one another. It teaches us how to treat each other. It teaches us how to deal with conflict. It teaches us how to watch out for the tricks of Satan who tries to deceive and destroy us using a plethora of traps including the ones I described earlier. The Bible teaches us about the consequences of not believing in God. The Bible warns us of both natural and eternal consequences for disobeying the laws and principles God has established. There are tons of benefits to reading, comprehending and applying biblical principles to your life so much so that the benefits are hard to quantify.

I see God as the ultimate parent. He only wants what's best for His children and He left us a manual that shows us how to get it. He warns us that this life will be filled with troubles and He tells us how to deal with trouble when it comes. It is unimaginable how someone could have access to such a great God and Father and neglect His love. I mean it's a pretty sweet benefits package if you ask me.

But I've been hurt by "CHURCH PEOPLE"

I know many people have been negatively impacted by people in the church, and unfortunately, many of those people have chosen to throw God away because of the actions of other flawed human beings. I don't know your specific situation or incident, but the reality is God didn't hurt you. He loves you and wants you to have a relationship with him. If you've been hurt or negatively impacted by people who claim they represent God, I'm sorry that happened. But remember, they are flawed human beings just like you and me. They are not God. Even those who are acting as direct representatives of God...are not God!

God uses broken, flawed beings as a witness and a mouthpiece to reach others. Perfection is neither a requirement nor a standard for being used by God. The only thing God requires is submission to Him through a relationship with Christ based on your faith in the saving work of Christ. If God required perfection of flawed human beings, there would be no one eligible for the job. With that in mind, please don't discard God because of what a flawed human being did. True believers in God try their best to live according to His instructions in the bible, but everyone messes up sometimes. Just as you need mercy for the times you mess up, consider showing mercy to others because, again, people are not perfect. John 3:16 states "for God so loved the world (in its entirety) that He gave His only begotten son that WHOSOEVER believes in Him shall have eternal life and shall not perish." This means you and I are qualified if we simply believe.

The Church. Is it relevant and necessary?

Yes. There I said it. Earthly indicators can confirm there is a God, but those indicators alone can't lead you into a relationship with Him. The way we get to know God on an intimate level is by studying the written word of God in the Bible. And where do you learn how to understand and properly interpret the word of God? You guessed it. The Church. Hearing the word of God allows us to understand our sin nature and embrace the need to repent. Without the teaching of the bible in church, there likely would be no conviction of wrongdoing because people wouldn't know how to tell when they were wrong. The church is the place we gather to build our faith, receive encouragement, instruction, correction, and to fellowship one with another. The church is the collective body of believers gathering under one common purpose which is to glorify God. Without the church community, I'm convinced the world would be far worse than it is now. The church has been a staple in the communities for thousands of years. It is still very much relevant and needed in order for us to live healthy, fulfilled, holistic lives where we support and grow with one another in the practice of our faith.

Closing remarks:

For those who chose to come along this bonus journey with me, I pray something was shared that added value to you, answered some spiritual questions, and maybe even gave you something to think about. I know asking questions about God and things that can be debatable can be difficult because of the strong opinions held by people. Sometimes asking such questions out loud can cause people to look at you weird or with the side eye.

I am a believer in Jesus and I want to share His love with everyone who is open to receiving it. His desire is to have a relationship with us and I want to use whatever platform I have to introduce many to Him for their benefit. As you can see from the book, my intent is to share with readers information that I believe to be valuable that can help them along this journey called life. It is my goal to fill in some of the gaps that were not taught to us in school, but needed to function in life outside of the classroom.

I hope you were blessed by this book. I poured everything I had in it with hopes of helping to add value to the readers life. I did my best to offer information, insight and wisdom from a place of humility that would help others in ways I wish I had years ago. Ignorance is expensive, and I've paid for it many times simply because I was UNDER-EDUCATED.

Please consider purchasing a copy of this book as a gift for your friends and family. Go and leave a positive review online and encourage others to read it. I'm on a mission to help at least one million people with this book. Will you help me? Will you commit to telling ten people about it? Will you share it on your social media platforms? Thanks in advance. God bless you. And thanks again for your support.

Made in the USA
Monee, IL
13 September 2026

62981001R00085